Stevia

naturally sweet recipes for desserts, drinks and more

by Rita DePuydt

Book Publishing Company
Summertown, Tennessee

Cover design: Warren Jefferson, Cynthia Holzapfel, Michael Cook
Interior design: Gwynelle Dismukes, Rita DePuydt
Photography: Warren Jefferson

Published in the United States by
Book Publishing Company
P.O. Box 99
Summertown, TN 38483
1-888-260-8458

Printed in the United States

ISBN10 1-57067-133-8   ISBN13 978-1-57067-133-3

15 14 13 12 11 10 09 08 07 06   9 8 7 6 5 4

DePuydt, Rita.
   Stevia : naturally sweet recipes for desserts, drinks, and more / by
Rita DePuydt.
        p. cm.
Includes index.
   ISBN 1-57067-133-8
   1. Cookery (Stevia) 2. Stevia rebaudiana. I. Title.
   TX819.S75 D4728 2002
   641.5'63--dc21

                              2002005270

*Recipes featured on the cover from upper left are:
Blueberry Muffins, p. 42;
Crepes, p. 111 with Apple Filling, p. 158
  and Berry Sauce, p 156;
Raspberry Cream, p. 32; Orange Cooler, p. 31;
Chocolate Cheesecake, p. 64.*

Calculations for the nutritional analyses in this book are based on the average number of servings listed with the recipes and the average amount of an ingredient if a range is called for. Calculations are rounded up to the nearest gram. If two options for an ingredient are listed, the first one is used. Not included are fat used for frying (unless the amount is specified in the recipe), optional ingredients, or serving suggestions.

TABLE OF CONTENTS

TABLE OF CONTENTS
(continued)

Acknowledgements

Producing this cookbook has been a fun, exciting, and very challenging experience. I would like to thank the following people who helped make this project a success. I really appreciate all their help.

A special thanks to my family and especially my parents, George and Mary DePuydt, for their tremendous support. And again, thanks to my Mom for sharing recipes and baking tips. A very big thanks to my brother, Ray, for the many hours of computer advice.

Thanks to my friends Lyn Duguid, Doug Davis, Heather Hewer, Lucy Colvin, Steven Hill, and Lisa Neulicht for their enduring and unwavering support. I'm also grateful to Evelyn Frament for her steady support, taste testing, recipe sharing, and advice.

A special thank you to Connie Rutherford for her computer help and for proofreading the book. I'm very grateful to Patt McDaniel for the generous use of her computer.

Thanks to Tony and Daphne Hallas for their professional assistance, generosity, and friendship. I'm especially grateful to designers Joe Papagni and Debi Spann for their expertise and great patience. I really appreciate the testing and editing work performed by Lisa Ashcroft from Wisdom Herbs. A big thanks to everyone at Kinko's in Ventura, California, and the Ojai Printing and Publishing Company for years of good service.

Thanks to Bob and Cynthia Holzapfel of the Book Publishing Company for taking an interest in my book and to the rest of the team for their creative efforts. I appreciate their integrity, fairness, and patience.

Thank You

Foreword

Stevia is the sweetener of the future! Now is the time to learn how to cook and bake with this health-promoting, incredibly sweet herb that contains no calories and has a **glycemic index of 0**. This revised edition incorporates the delicious recipes contained in the former Volumes I and II of *Baking with Stevia* and adds several new recipes. Rita routinely bakes with these recipes, which utilize stevia extract powder (a white crystalline powder extracted from the leaves of the stevia plant), whole-leaf stevia concentrate, and ground stevia leaf. Each of these forms of stevia has a different ratio of sweetness compared to sugar. So follow the recipes carefully. Stevia, in any of its consumable forms, does not adversely affect blood sugar, and therefore may be used freely by people with diabetes or hypoglycemia. The whole-leaf stevia, besides being sweet, is remarkably nutritious, while the stevia extract is incredibly sweet (about 200 to 300 times sweeter than sugar).

You will love these recipes. Best of all, when eating or drinking the foods and beverages, you can be assured that stevia has made them more nutritious and better for the health and well-being of every member of your family. Many experts believe that stevia is the safest sweetener known to man, and it is recommended by many nutritionists.

Stevia is an incredible plant. It is not only safe to use, it is good for you and adds no calories to your food. It does not make you crave more of it, as do some artificial sweeteners. In fact stevia tends to reduce one's cravings for sweets and at the same time improves oral health. The leaves of a good-quality plant are about 30 times sweeter than sugar. These recipes not only provide the wonderful natural sweetness of stevia but its marvelous healing benefits as well. When cooking with whole-leaf stevia products, it is important to be aware that stevia leaves from China may not be as sweet and may not have quite the same delightful flavor of Paraguayan stevia, thereby requiring more ground leaf. When using the stevia extract powder (white stevioside) look for a brand that contains at least 90% steviosides.

I was pleased when Rita asked me to write the foreword to this revised volume of her *Baking with Stevia* recipes. I have been using stevia daily since my introduction to it in 1982. I have worked continuously with both the Guarani Indian farmers and Paraguayan agricultural officials to improve both the quality and quantity of their stevia production. I have importuned many congressmen and other United States Government officials in order to increase the availability of this remarkable herb in America. Stevia is one of the Paraguayan herbs that have become my passion. I love stevia. I love its taste and what it does within the human body. I have just completed a book entitled *The Miracle of Stevia*. As you learn to use this delightful herb, you too will come to love it and be grateful for stevia and its numerous health-restoring properties.

Uses for high-quality ground stevia leaf are as varied as your imagination. Try it as a sweet spice on cooking vegetables. Sprinkle it into soups, cereals, salads, barbecue and pasta sauces, stews, and chili. Blend it with ground cinnamon for a delicious cinnamon and stevia toast. Make your own sweet liquid from the stevia tea bags and use that in cooking or baking, or make ice cubes to sweeten other beverages. Children love a stevia popsicle. Stevia makes good food better—and more nutritious! In addition to all of the sweet compounds, Stevia leaves contain numerous vitamins and minerals, including beta-carotene, vitamin C, austroinulin (nourishes the good bacteria in our intestines), calcium, chromium, cobalt, iron, magnesium, manganese, niacin, phosphorus, potassium, protein, selenium, silicon, sodium, and zinc.

Where else will you find an herb, in its natural form, that is deliciously sweet but will nourish your pancreas and help to restore and maintain a normal blood sugar level, and even help to lower high blood pressure? Where else will you find a sweet tasting herb that helps to destroy harmful bacteria, reduce cavities, and helps to stop bleeding gums? Where else will you find an herb that, in its natural liquid concentrate form, is as healing to the skin as it is to the internal body?

When you discover some of the many uses and health benefits of the various forms of this sweet tasting herb, it will become your passion. For the health of your family, you will settle for nothing less than stevia. You will love Rita's stevia recipes and will soon be developing your own. Nature gave us this incredible plant. Enjoy the sweetness and health that is stevia.

James A. May
President, Wisdom Herbs™ Company
and author of The Miracle of Stevia

Stevia

naturally sweet recipes
for desserts, drinks
and more

Introduction

This revised edition of *Baking with Stevia I and II* (now called *Stevia; Naturally Sweet Recipes for Desserts, Drinks, and More*) not only uses a white powdered extract as a primary sweetener, but also introduces the cook to a number of other stevia products, including clear liquid extract, stevia extract with filler, dried green herb, and a dark liquid concentrate. (See pages 10-12 for descriptions.) Stevia is extremely useful and healthful in all of its forms.

The leaves of the South American shrub *Stevia rebaudiana* contain several molecular compounds that are extremely sweet tasting. The white powdered and clear liquid stevia extracts are purified concentrates of these sweet-tasting molecules known as *glycosides*. A number of glycosides have been isolated from the plant, including *stevioside* and *rebaudioside*.

These extracts are approximately 200 to 300 times sweeter than sugar. The dried whole green herb, though less sweet than the extract (about 10 to 30 times sweeter than sugar), retains all the medicinal attributes of the herb and contributes a pleasant sweetness to many foods. Herbal concentrates combine the medicinal properties of the whole herb (intensified) with a higher sweetening capability than the dried herb. The taste of stevia is not identical to sugar, but has a flavor more like nectar or licorice.

In addition to the sweet glycoside molecules found in stevia (primarily stevioside), there is also a bitter component. There is a direct correlation between bitterness and leaf quality. Environmental factors including soil, water, sunlight, air quality, farming practices, processing, and storage can all influence the percent of sweet glycosides and other qualities found in the leaf. The bitter taste is particularly evident in the powdered extracts. However, when appropriately diluted for consumption in a beverage or in baked goods, the bitter flavor disappears. Some companies are researching ways to eliminate this bitter element.

The amount of stevioside in an extract varies depending on the source, though it is generally between 85% and 95%. Sweetening potencies vary among different brands and even within the same brand. In this book I used an extract from Wisdom Herbs which seems to be of a potency in the middle range, about 90%. **Approximately ⅓ to ½ teaspoon of powdered extract has the sweetening capability of one cup of sugar, while about ½ teaspoon of clear liquid extract equals one cup of sugar.** A clear liquid or white powdered extract may be used interchangeably in the following recipes.

Many people prefer using a clear liquid extract because they can carry a bottle around in their purses or briefcases, and it dissolves easily in liquids. A liquid form can be made from the powder. (See pages 11-12.)

Some powdered extracts on the market are mixed with a filler such as maltodextrin or FOS (see glossary, page 191, for definitions). For the most part, I only use pure extracts without filler. I do use an extract with an FOS filler to shake on oatmeal or into a blender drink. I have experimented with it in my recipes and found that stevia with FOS filler doesn't make a qualitative difference in the product and is expensive to use in baking. It may help cookies, muffins, cakes, puddings, etc., but I have not been able to ascertain the difference. I have never used an extract with maltodextrin filler so I can't tell how it affects cooking and baking. If you use stevia extract with filler, follow the same recipes but use the equivalency listed on page 177. If things are coming out dry or the batter is too thick, then reduce the flour by 1 or 2 tablespoons or add a small amount more liquid.

The whole leaf, dried and powdered, may also be added to many recipes, such as breads and muffins, for sweetening and added health benefits. The powdered form can be added directly to foods, and the liquid from stevia tea may be used in place of other liquids in a recipe. There is a point, however, where the addition of powdered leaf will turn bakery items green and an herb (or grassy) flavor may predominate. In general this happens after the addition of more than 1 tablespoon. This may not bother some people.

I also use a thick, dark stevia concentrate to replace molasses or brown sugar in a recipe. It works very well to use a combination of the herb or herbal concentrate with a white powder or liquid extract. Also a "green" extract can be made from the leaves at home. (See page 15 to make your own extract.)

Such a small amount of stevia is needed to sweeten a recipe that adjustments were made to replace the bulk and characteristics of regular sweeteners. I relied on applesauce, apple butter, fruits, and nut butters when developing these recipes. Applesauce and apple butter work well; they don't have an over-powering flavor, and unsweetened brands are generally available everywhere. However, other fruit sauces and fruit butters (or purées) can be substituted for variety in flavor. Peach, pear, or plum sauce could be used, as well as baby food. Berry and other fruit purées are also available.

This collection of recipes relies on stevia's property as a flavor enhancer—it sweetens and brings out the flavors of other foods. Numerous recipes in this book take advantage of the wonderful flavors and other qualities of fresh and dried fruit, which are greatly enlivened by using stevia. In some recipes, one or two tablespoons of a natural sweetener, such as date sugar, rice syrup, maple syrup, or honey, were added. The stevia picks up on this small amount of sweetener and magnifies it. I prefer these sweeteners to sugar (sucrose, fructose, and brown sugar), but if you are accustomed to using sugar and want to substitute a tablespoon or two for my suggestions, do so.

You may wish to reduce the suggested sweeteners or eliminate them altogether. **If you are unable to tolerate the sweeteners suggested in this book, then simply eliminate them from the recipes.** The small amount suggested has a minimal effect on the overall success of the baked goods. It might not work to eliminate the sweetener suggested in the chocolate recipes and some of the cake and frosting recipes, but you can try. (See pages 180-81 for further discussion.) My goal is to keep carbohydrate-based sweeteners to a minimum, yet achieve good taste, texture, and appearance.

Stevia is stable at high temperatures well over the boiling point, and in acidic foods. These properties make stevia easy to work with. You will not have to be concerned about boiling stevia too long or baking at too high a temperature. It can be mixed into any type of food. If you are steeping tea bags to derive sweetness and medicinal properties, there is no need to boil the herb. Keep the temperature below the boiling point to avoid destroying other nutrients.

I have attempted to provide a broad range of dessert and beverage recipes and to show the various ways the different stevia products can be used. I have included many classic and popular recipes that have been enhanced by using only fresh, whole, natural ingredients. In this revised volume, many of the original recipes have been improved; the fat content in some of the recipes has been reduced, and a number of simpler recipes have been developed for the busy cook. Where possible, I give a choice of ingredients. Many of the ingredients can be purchased at the grocery store, others at fruit and nut shops or gourmet food stores. Some of the ingredients are only available at health food stores.

A nutritional analysis for each recipe is provided that will be helpful for people with diabetes, those concerned about calories, and others keeping track of fat, protein, and carbohydrate grams in their food. Also, this edition has a new section on growing your own stevia plants that includes uses for the fresh leaves.

Keep in mind that products made with stevia will not taste like those made with a lot of sugar. But high quality, pleasant-tasting goods can be produced. Remember that it is easy to add too much stevia extract, which overwhelms the taste buds. Use it judiciously.

Stevia is excellent for anyone who wishes to reduce the amount of regular or artificial sweeteners in their diet. If you wish to eliminate the extra empty calories sugar supplies and are concerned about the negative health effects of sugar or artificial sweeteners, then stevia is the perfect choice. Whether you just want to cut down on sugars or you can't have any sweeteners at all, the various stevia products can greatly assist you in your program. Enjoy exploring the uses of this wonderful herb in your daily life.

Rita DePuydt

Stevia Facts

- Stevia comes in two basic forms:

  1. Natural dried green leaves (crushed or powdered) and dark herbal extracts of the leaves. The leaves are about 10 to 30 times sweeter than sugar.

  2. Pure stevioside extracts of stevia in a white powder or clear liquid that are 200 to 300 times sweeter than sugar.

- Some white powdered stevia extracts on the market today contain a filler made of either maltodextrin or fructooligo-saccharides (FOS).

- The sweet taste in stevia comes from glycoside molecules that have 0 calories and are not carbohydrates.

- The sweetness of stevia leaves and pure extracts varies from source to source and among the different brands. The genetics of the plant, cultivation, and processing all influence the stevioside content.

- The whole leaf products contain all the health benefits of the herb. Some research shows that pure stevioside extracts may have health benefits. More research in this area in needed.

- There is no known toxicity associated with stevia herb or stevioside extracts. Extensive safety and toxicity testing have been performed, and stevia has always been shown to be safe.

- Stevia has a bitter component that can be reduced by proper cultiva-tion and processing. Some products claim to be less bitter than others.

- Stevia extracts can be purchased in the United States as a dietary supplement.

- Some stevia is grown in Paraguay and Canada, but most is grown in China.

History and Health Benefits of Stevia

The herb *Stevia rebaudiana* has been used for centuries by the Guarani Indians of Paraguay, who have several names for the plant, including *Ka'a-he'e, Ca'a-e'he,* or *Ca-a-yupe,* all referring to the sweet leaf or "honey leaf." It is commonly known in South America as *yerba dulce,* meaning sweet herb. The Guarani have used stevia nutritionally and medicinally.

The plant came to the attention of the rest of the world when the South American naturalist Bertoni "discovered" the plant in the late 1800s. After his report, the herb became widely used by herbalists in Paraguay.

Stevia's most obvious and notable characteristic is its sweet taste. However, the sweet taste is not due to carbohydrate-based molecules, but to several non-caloric molecules called *glycosides.* Individuals who cannot tolerate sugar or other sweeteners can use stevia. The first glycoside molecule, named *stevioside,* was isolated from stevia in 1931 by two French chemists named Bridel and Lavieille.

During WW II, sugar shortages prompted England to begin investigation of stevia for use as a sweetener. Cultivation began under the direction of the Royal Botanical Gardens at Kew, but the project was abandoned in the aftermath of the war. Numerous countries have discovered stevia in the past several decades. Japan began cultivating stevia in hothouses in the 1950s, and has done extensive research and safety testing on the plant. This testing has shown the herb and its extracts to be non-toxic, safe for people with diabetes, and beneficial in cases of obesity. In addition, stevia is not a source of nutrition for bacteria in the mouth or candida yeast in the colon.

By the l970s, Japan started using stevia commercially. Today, they are the biggest users of the extract, which comprises 50% of Japan's sweetener industry. In Japan, stevia is used commercially in prepared foods such as chewing gum, candy, soft drinks, juices, frozen desserts, low-calorie foods, and baked goods.

With the average sugar consumption in the United States at 150 pounds per person per year, this country would benefit greatly from a healthy natural sweetener like stevia. Currently stevia is sold in the United States only as a dietary supplement and in skin care products. Despite years of safety and toxicity testing in other countries, the FDA has not approved the use of stevia as a sweetener in the U.S.

Other aspects of stevia are attracting people's attention. The herb is sold in some South American countries to aid people with diabetes or hypoglycemia. Research has shown that a whole-leaf concentrate has a regulating effect on the pancreas and helps stabilize blood sugar levels.

Other traditional uses of the stevia herb include lowering elevated blood pressure (hypertension), aiding digestion by reducing gas and stomach acidity, relieving nausea, and helping to reduce obesity. The herb acts as a general tonic that increases energy levels and mental acuity.

Stevia has been shown to inhibit the growth and reproduction of bacteria that cause gum disease and tooth decay, making it an excellent addition to toothpastes and mouthwashes. Many people have reported improvement in their oral health after adding stevia concentrate to their toothpaste and using it, diluted in water, as a daily mouthwash.

Stevia is useful in healing a number of skin problems. Whole stevia concentrate may be applied as a facial mask to soften and tighten the skin and smooth out wrinkles. Smooth the dark liquid over the entire face, allowing it to dry for at least 30 to 60 minutes. A drop of concentrate may be applied directly to any blemish, acne outbreak, or lip or mouth sore. Stevia concentrate is also effective when used on seborrhea, dermatitis, and eczema. Stevia concentrate is reported to heal cuts and scratches more rapidly when applied to the affected area.

Stevia concentrate added to soap eliminates dandruff and other scalp problems and improves the health and luster of the hair. It also helps to retain natural hair color.

It is unknown at this time whether the glycoside extracts of stevia have health benefits attributable just to them, although two recent studies indicate there may be some. A study in Denmark found that stevioside enhances insulin secretion from mouse pancreatic islets in the presence of glucose. According to researchers, glycoside extract of stevia "stimulates insulin secretion via a direct action on pancreatic beta cells." Another study in Taiwan showed that stevioside reduced blood pressure in hypertensive subjects. As more studies take place around the world and more people use the herb, the healing properties attributed to stevia will be examined and clarified.

Refined sugar consumption continues to rise in the United States. According to the Center for Science in the Public Interest (Nov. 1998), sugar consumption has risen by 25 pounds per person since 1986 to 152 pounds per person per year (calculated from sugar production figures). Sugar displaces nutritive calories, leading to numerous health problems and obesity. A major factor contributing to this high rate of sugar consumption is the widespread and continually growing habit of drinking sugar-laden soda pops.

This review of the therapeutic properties of stevia in no way constitutes an endorsement of such uses by the author or the publisher. If you are under a doctor's care, please consult a qualified physician before experimenting with this herb.

Stevia Products and Uses

There are a number of stevia products now on the market of two basic types: whole herb products and purified extracts. Below are descriptions of the currently available products.

STEVIA TEA BAGS

* Drink stevia tea in convenient flow-thru bags by itself, or blend with other herbs. Delicious hot or cold.
* Use stevia tea to replace other liquids in a recipe.
* Stevia tea, alone or blended with other herbs or juice, may be frozen to make a flavorful and nutritious popsicle.
* Stevia tea can provide quick relief for upset stomach and nausea.
* Used bags may be dabbed on the face or placed over the eyes for a few minutes to smooth and tighten the skin.
* Add stevia tea bags to any liquid that you want to sweeten.

STEVIA LEAF, POWDERED OR CUT AND SIFTED

Dried stevia leaves may be used to enhance the flavor and nutritional value of many foods. They can be 10 to 30 times sweeter than sugar. The dried leaves can be purchased in a fine powder or in larger pieces called cut, or cut and sifted. Try these suggestions.

* Add to pasta sauce, sweet and sour sauce, and barbecue sauce.
* Add to salads, salad dressings, and potato salad.
* Sprinkle over steamed vegetables or baked potatoes.
* Use in soup, stew, chili, baked beans, pizza, and stir fries.

* Mix with cinnamon in a shaker to sprinkle on toast or cereal.
* Bake into bread, rolls, and muffins.

STEVIA CONCENTRATE

The concentrate is made by carefully cooking stevia leaves in water to make a dark, syrupy liquid. It is stable for months, and the flavor seems to improve with age.
* Use in place of molasses or brown sugar in recipes such as molasses cookies, pumpkin pie, pumpkin bars, or spice cake.
* Apply as a facial mask to smooth and tighten the skin.
* Inhibits the growth of bacteria that cause tooth decay and gum disease.

STEVIA POWDERED EXTRACT

A white powder containing only the sweet glycoside molecules extracted from stevia leaves—a highly concentrated form generally 200 to 300 times sweeter than sugar. Does not adversely affect blood glucose levels. This is a pure extract that does not contain a filler such as maltodextrin.
* Useful in all baked goods, including pies, cakes, cookies, and muffins.
* Excellent in beverages.
* Superb in puddings, gelled foods, and frozen desserts.
* Enhances the flavors of fruit. Fruit salads come alive.

STEVIA CLEAR LIQUID EXTRACT

Contains a stevia powdered extract dissolved in water. It will not keep long without a preservative. (Commercial products generally contain one.) The liquid extract is interchangeable with powdered extract.

To make liquid extract from the powder, mix 1 teaspoon powder to 3 tablespoons purified water. Keep in a clean 1-ounce dropper bottle.

* Easy to use, convenient for carrying in a purse or when traveling.
* Excellent for beverages of all types, including coffee, tea, home-made soda pop, and smoothies.

STEVIA EXTRACT BLENDED WITH A FILLER

Several companies sell a powdered extract that is blended with a filler such as maltodextrin or fructooligosaccharides (FOS). These are found in individual packets or in shaker bottles and were designed to make stevia easier to measure and use. Products with FOS as a filler are preferred, since FOS itself is a valuable nutritional supplement that provides nourishment for the friendly bacteria in the colon. The amount of stevia in these products varies from company to company. In general approximately **1½ to 2 tablespoons of extract with filler equals ½ teaspoon pure stevia extract**. I did not use this product in this recipe book; however, experimentation has shown that you will have good luck directly substituting this product at the above ratio in most of the recipes.

NOTES: To take advantage of the full health benefits of stevia, use the whole dried herb, or herbal concentrate. One or two teaspoons of the concentrate and up to a tablespoon of the herb may be added to the muffins, cakes, cookies, and bars in the recipes if desired.

If you don't care for the herb taste or green color in your products, use the purified extract, either the white powder or the clear liquid. A combination of one of the herb products with an extract can be used with good success.

Bringing Out the Sweetness of Stevia

If you are accustomed to sugary baked goods, stevia-sweetened foods may not seem sweet enough at first. You can try adding a little more stevia than the recipe calls for, but too much stevia overwhelms the taste buds and does not improve the sweetness or flavor. It works better to try some methods that use the ability of stevia to enhance flavors.

I have also sometimes noticed that baked goods taste sweeter the next day, or after they have been frozen, than they do when they first come out of the oven.

Try these tips to improve on the sweetness and flavor of your baked foods. Soon you may be overwhelmed by the taste of sugar-laden desserts.

✦ Utilize fruit, fruit juices, fruit sauces and purées, and dairy products in your recipes. Add a tablespoon or two of frozen fruit juice concentrate to recipes to add flavor and zing. Stevia enhances their natural sugars and flavors.

✦ Soak cranberries or other fruit in stevia extract for 15 minutes to several hours, or even overnight prior to use. The fruit gets sweeter as it soaks.

✦ When softening or stewing dried fruit in juice or water, mix the stevia extract in with it.

✦ While thawing frozen berries, mix a little stevia extract into them in the bowl or cup.

+ Add 1 or 2 teaspoons of powdered dried stevia herb to batter for extra sweetness and flavor.

+ Replace some or all of the liquid in a recipe with stevia tea (an infusion of stevia leaves in hot water).

+ Refrigerate or freeze cookie dough for 4 hours to overnight before baking. The dough will handle better and taste sweeter.

+ Refrigerate or freeze baked goods. Cut up into individual servings and freeze. Freshen up in the microwave for about 30 seconds.

+ Add 1 to 3 tablespoons of another sweetener such as date sugar, malt syrup, or honey. The stevia will enhance these natural sweeteners. **Disregard this suggestion if you can't have any sweeteners.**

Making Stevia Extract

Heat 2 cups of purified water almost to the boiling point. Remove the pan from the heat, add ¼ cup of finely crushed or powdered dried stevia leaves, and stir. Cover and steep the herb overnight. If steeping in a pan, use glass or enamel. Pour the liquid extract off from the settled herbs in the bottom of the pan, then strain the liquid through a cheesecloth. Place the cheesecloth inside a strainer and pour over a bowl or pan. More of the herb powder will settle to the bottom. Don't mix it in. Pour the extract off, if you prefer. The extract has a better flavor once all the powder has settled. Keep in a covered container in the refrigerator. The extract will be dark greenish black in color.

This method of extraction produces the most pleasant-tasting extract. It is less bitter than an extract that has been cooked by simmering or boiling and has a nice, sweet, licorice-like taste. It is not a very concentrated sweetener, however. It takes about 1 or 2 tablespoons of extract to sweeten 1 cup of tea. This can vary a lot depending on the stevioside content of the herb.

To make a stronger concentrate. let the tea stand for several minutes, then pour the liquid extract off from the sediment in the bottom. Simmer the liquid on very low heat in an uncovered pan until reduced by half. Keep refrigerated. The extract will be twice as strong but may become more bitter.

Growing Stevia

Many people are interested in growing stevia in their gardens, on their patios, or in the house. And why not? It's a great plant to have around. Like so many other herbs that you cherish and enjoy, stevia would be a welcome addition to your garden and your kitchen.

Culinary uses for the fresh leaves of stevia are still being explored. With their fresh, gentle sweetness, surely these leaves will lead to some delightful discoveries. Several leaves or a small sprig make a wonderful garnish on the dinner plate or as an after-dinner palate pleaser. The leaves are attractive and can be placed on the side or rim of a desert cup with pudding, custard, or ice cream. Leaves can be served on the rim of a glass of iced tea or lemonade. Stevia combines well with mint, so any recipe that calls for fresh mint leaves can be complemented with fresh stevia leaves. Fresh stevia may enhance recipes for chutney, fresh salsa, or other sauces, fruit and other salads. Some people find that the leaves have to be dried (crushed or powdered) for the sweetness to be noticed in food, since the flavors of other foods dominate fresh stevia leaves. The experimentation and discoveries are yours to pursue.

The information presented here on growing stevia is not derived from personal experience. I have several plants overwintering in pots in the house, but I am a beginner when it come to growing stevia. The first thing I noticed with the starts I bought at the local nursery is that they don't seem to have a high stevioside content. I was disappointed when 10 fresh leaves had no sweetening effect on a cup of tea. Then I dried some leaves and used about 20 in a cup of tea—nothing. My next step will be to buy some new starts with a known stevioside content.

Stevia is considered easy to grow but has a few basic requirements. The following information is adapted from a growing guide prepared and shared by Mulberry Creek Herb Farm of Ohio (see Sources, page 21) with additions from an Internet article titled "Growing Stevia rebaudiana," by Jeffrey Goettemoeller, author of *Stevia Sweet Recipes*.

Stevia rebaudiana is one of 154 members of the genus *Stevia*. A member of the sunflower family (*Asteraceae*, formerly *Compositae*), stevia is a small herbaceous subtropical perennial shrub that grows to be 2 to 3 feet tall. The plant has alternate leaves, small white flowers, and small seeds that are dispersed in the wind via a hairy pappus. Native to the mountains of northeastern Paraguay and adjacent sections of Brazil, stevia grows best in cooler climates. During the growing season it thrives in a temperature range of 60 to 85 degrees. It grows as a perennial in frost-free zones but otherwise can be grown as an annual, as are most commercially grown crops. The leaves of the shrub contain diterpene glycoside molecules that are extremely sweet-tasting. The four major glycosides are stevioside, rebaudioside A and C, and dulcoside A. The exact purpose of these compounds in the plant is not yet clear. This is the only member of the genus containing the sweet compounds. The dried leaves are about 10 to 30 times sweeter than sugar while the stevioside extracts are 200 to 300 times sweeter.

Sources for Plants and Seeds

Find a local source of stevia plants if you can because the plants may not ship well. If you are unsuccessful in locating stevia in your area, several companies in the U.S. and Canada will ship starter plants. Try to determine if your plants have been grown from cuttings with a high stevioside content, and find a new source if your starts turn out to be low in stevioside. Seeds are more difficult to find, though several companies do carry them. The quality of the seed in terms of viability and stevioside content may be unreliable. (See the list of sources on page 21.)

When to Get Started

In most areas, stevia will be grown as an annual. Plant it outside in early spring after all danger of frost has passed—two weeks after the last frost date. To begin earlier, start the plants indoors. You can then use cold frames or plastic covers outside to harden the plants off for several weeks before transplanting. The hardening-off process is used to gradually expose tender seedlings to the natural elements.

Planting dates in the southern states are determined more by day length than last frost date. Stevia requires a minimum of 12 hours of sunlight to remain green and growing. If the plants don't get enough light, they will start to flower. Plant when there is 12 hours of light and the soil temperatures are in the 50s or 60s.

Preferred Exposure

Full sun is preferred but not hot weather. Stevia is very adaptable to most areas of the U.S. and southern Canada. Day length is more critical than light intensity. Filtered afternoon shade from noon to 4 P.M. will be required in the southern states of the U.S. during the hot summer months.

Soil Conditions

Stevia prefers well-draining sandy loam or loam, high in organic matter. Basically, you need a good garden soil similar to that in a cultivated vegetable garden; heavy clay soils do not work. Add compost to enrich the soil. Raised beds work well. Apply a layer of mulch such as straw or bark after the weather is consistently warm. This will keep the roots cool and the leaves clean, preserve water, and hold down the weeds. Be very careful when weeding around mature plants as their brittle branches are easily broken.

Watering

Stevia requires a consistently moist soil, not waterlogged. Avoid over-watering or letting the plants dry out. If the tips of the plants start to droop, it is time to water. Keep evenly moist with frequent light watering, especially during summer heat. A drip or soaker hose is effective. Don't plant in areas subject to flooding or puddling.

Fertilizer

Use a balanced, slow-release organic fertilizer or manure which is tilled into the soil before planting. Avoid high-nitrogen chemical fertilizers as they produce large leaves with little flavor.

Harvesting and Drying Stevia

Harvest in the morning for highest glycoside content. If grown as an annual, the full harvest will occur in late September or early October (before the first frost—protect if necessary). The cool fall nights intensify glycoside production but once flowering has begun, sweetness in the leaves declines. Removing flowering heads is not effective. Failure to harvest plants before the flowers have opened up will allow these flowers to impart a bitter flavor to the leaves.

To harvest, cut the entire plant at the base. Use leaves fresh or dry by either of the following methods.

With a rubber band or string, tie bunches of stems together and hang upside down to dry under warm, dark conditions with adequate airflow. When dry, remove the leaves from the stems. Another method is to remove the leaves from the stems and lay them out on a screen in a warm dark place. Keep air flowing through the top and bottom of the screen. You may also use a home dehydrator.

Store the dried herb in zip-lock baggies or glass jars. Use the herb crushed or grind the dried leaves into a powder in a coffee grinder, blender, or food processor. A liquid extract can also be made by soaking ¼ cup dried herb in 2 cups of hot water for 12 hours. Strain with a fine-mesh strainer lined with a cheesecloth. Keep the extract refrigerated.

If re-growth of the plant is desired, leave at least 4 inches on the plant when harvesting, and it will come back the following year.

Propagation

Stevia is a perennial and in frost-free climates can be grown as such;

however, the plants decline after several years. If you are growing stevia as an annual or if your perennial shrub has lost its flavor, cuttings can be taken and new plants started. Cuttings should be 2 to 4 inches long with at least 2 leaf buds. Remove all but 2 to 3 leaves. The cuttings can be rooted in a glass of water (in about 4 days) or the ends can be dipped in rooting hormones and planted in rooting medium (vermiculite) for 2 to 4 weeks in small cell packs. Once roots have formed, plant the cuttings in 4- to 5-inch pots in a light potting soil and grow another 2 to 4 weeks. Keep in a sunny location until spring. Grow lights or fluorescent lights can be used.

General Growing Instructions

Plant in rows 1½ to 2 feet apart with 1½ feet between plants in the row 2 weeks after all danger of frost is past.

Keep the soil evenly moist.

Pinch tips of stems every 3 to 4 weeks for several months. This will encourage side branching producing bushier plants. (Dry and use these pinched leaves.)

After the last pinching, mulch with straw or bark. This should be just before the summer heat.

Harvest the entire plant as flower buds begin to appear. Stevioside levels begin to drop as the plant flowers. Short fall days trigger blossoming.

Southern Growing Instructions

Follow the instructions above but put the plants out once the day length has reached at least 12 hours and soil temperatures have warmed up to 50 to 60 degrees.

Plants must have filtered afternoon shade during the hot summer months. Find an area in the yard that is naturally shaded in the afternoon, or use some type of shade cloth.

Container Growing

Stevia can be grown in containers in your yard, porch, balcony, or in the house. Use a container 12 to 14 inches across. A double pot system works well with a plastic pot covered by a larger decorative pot. The air space between the pots will keep the soil cooler in direct, hot sun.

For soil, mix a little garden soil into the potting soil in the bottom half of the pot to hold water and fertilizer better. Fill the rest of the container with potting soil. Mulch the top of the container with bark or sphagnum moss as the summer approaches.

Keep plants evenly moist. Never let them completely dry out.

In southern states, move containers from the south side of the house to the east side in the summer and return to the south side in the fall.

Fertilize every 2 to 3 weeks with a slow-release, organic fertilizer. Too much of any fertilizer will result in large, flavorless leaves.

Stevia may be grown indoors in a sunny window or using grow lights. Remember a total of 12 hours of light is required to keep plants from flowering.

Sources

Plants

Mulberry Creek Herb Farm
3312 Bogart Rd.
Huron, OH 44839
(419) 433-6126
www.mulberrycreek.com
Starter plants in 3-inch pots

Herbal Advantage
131 Bobwhite Rd.
Rogersville, MO 65742
(800) 753-9199
www.herbaladvantage.com
Starter plants in 2-inch pots

Seeds

Seeds from Around the World
Jim Johnson, 3421 Bream St.
Gautier, MS 39553
(800) 336-2064
www.seedman.com

Park Seed Co.
1 Parkton Ave.
Greenwood, SC 29649
(800) 213-0076
www.parkseed.com

Notes about Additional Sweeteners in the Recipes

Several of the recipes in this book call for additional sweeteners, such as date sugar, maple syrup, molasses, or honey. In most cases these sweeteners are optional and are marked as such in the ingredients lists. These ingredients are included in the directions, but if you choose not to use additional sweeteners, simply disregard them. In some recipes, the additional sweeteners are necessary to achieve the desired flavor and/or consistency of the dish.

If two options for an ingredient are listed, the first one is used in calculating the nutritional analysis. Not included are optional ingredients or serving suggestions.

Beverages

Helpful Hints

* Stevia is great for beverages of all kinds. You can carry a small bottle of liquid extract with you to use in your coffee or tea. If you have powdered extract, it's easy to make a liquid form. Just mix 1 teaspoon of powdered extract into 3 tablespoons of purified water. Pour into a small clean dropper bottle. Commercial liquid extracts have some type of preservative (usually grapefruit seed extract). Don't make up too much ahead and throw it out if you see mold or if it tastes bad after a week or so. Refrigeration will increase the shelf life.

* I use the powdered stevia extract in this book. You can substitute commercial liquid extract in all the recipes. It is easier to blend a liquid into beverages like lemonade or punch. If you are using powdered extract mix it into a small amount of water first to dissolve it more readily and add that to the beverage.

* Use the lower amount of stevia listed in the recipe at first and add more to taste if necessary. Stevia products vary so much in stevioside content (sweetness), usually ranging from 85% to about 95%. The sweetness can even vary within the same brand.

* Tofu is measured by weight in these recipes.

* When measuring liquid stevia from a dropper, use the following formula:

  60 drops = 1 teaspoon

❧ MINT STEVIA ICED TEA

Stevia and mint make perfect partners

Yield:
1 quart
(4 servings)

Per serving:
Calories 0
Total Fat 0 g
Sat. Fat 0 g
Protein 0 g
Carb. 0 g
Fiber 0 g
Sodium 0 mg

2 **stevia tea bags** (2 teaspoons crushed dried leaf)
2 mint tea bags (1 tablespoon crushed dried leaf)
1 quart purified water

• Place the tea bags or loose tea in a quart jar filled with purified water. Cover and place in the refrigerator for 8 to 12 hours. Remove the tea bags or strain if using loose herbs. Serve in tall glasses over ice.

❧ LEMONADE

Now, a sugar-free version of this old favorite

Yield:
1 quart
(4 servings)

Per serving:
Calories 11
Total Fat 0 g
Sat. Fat 0 g
Protein 0 g
Carb. 4 g
Fiber 0.2 g
Sodium 0.1 mg

6 ounces of lemon juice (3 to 4 lemons)
Purified water to make a quart
⅓ to ½ teaspoon **powdered stevia extract** (to taste)

• Juice the lemons and strain. If some or all of the pulp is desired then use it. Place the juice in a quart glass jar or pitcher, and fill with water. Add stevia extract to taste. Chill in the refrigerator. Stays fresh and pleasant-tasting for several days.

Ginger Ale

Try this stimulating and tasteful beverage at home.

¼ cup peeled and sliced fresh gingerroot
½ lemon or 1 small lime, sliced
4 cups water
⅓ to ½ teaspoon **powdered stevia extract** (to taste)
1 quart chilled sparkling mineral water

• Peel and slice the ginger. Slice the lemon or lime into ¼-inch circles. Place the ginger and citrus in the water in a pan, and simmer for 20 to 30 minutes.

• Strain the liquid into a glass jar or other container. Stir in the stevia extract to taste and refrigerate.

• To serve, pour about equal amounts of the ginger water and chilled sparkling water into a glass. If using lemon or lime flavored sparkling water, omit simmering the lemon or lime slices with the ginger.

NOTE: *Simmer only! Do not bring ginger to a boil because it will become bitter.*

OPTION: *Add several stevia herbal tea bags during the last 10 minutes of simmering instead of using the stevia extract.*

Yield:
about 2
quarts
(8 servings)

Per serving:
Calories 3
Total Fat 0 g
Sat. Fat 0 g
Protein 0 g
Carb. 1 g
Fiber .2 g
Sodium 2 mg

 # ORANGE POP

A cool, light, and refreshing thirst-quencher

2 cups fresh orange juice (6 to 8 oranges)
1½ cups purified water
⅓ to ½ teaspoon **powdered stevia extract** (to taste)
8 to 12 ounces chilled sparkling water (flavored or unflavored)

• Squeeze the oranges and strain out the pulp. Mix in the water and stevia extract. Cover and chill in the refrigerator.

• Pour about 7 ounces of the chilled juice into four 12-ounce glasses. Add 2 to 3 ounces of sparkling water to each glass just before serving. Best if used in 1 to 2 days.

NOTE: *If sparkling water is unavailable, use another 8 to 12 ounces of chilled regular water to make a pleasant orangeade.*

Yield:
4 servings

Per serving:
Calories 56
Total Fat 0 g
Sat. Fat 0 g
Protein 1 g
Carb. 13 g
Fiber .2 g
Sodium 2 mg

❈ QUICK CRANBERRY PUNCH

Sparkling fresh and alive—sure to jazz up any party

12 ounces frozen unsweetened cran-apple juice concentrate
½ to ¾ teaspoon **powdered stevia extract** (to taste)
2 quarts chilled sparkling water (flavored or unflavored)
Slices of oranges and lemons (optional)

• Place the frozen juice concentrate and stevia extract in a large punch bowl or pitcher. Add the sparkling water to the punch bowl just before serving. Float round slices of oranges and/or lemons on the surface of the bowl, if desired.

VARIATION: *Also excellent with a cran-raspberry juice blend concentrate.*

Yield:
8 servings

Per serving:
Calories 30
Total Fat 0 g
Sat. Fat 0 g
Protein 0 g
Carb. 8 g
Fiber 0 g
Sodium 3 mg

STRAWBERRY PINA SMOOTHIE

Transport yourself to a warm, tropical beach with coconut palms swaying in the breeze.

3 cups unsweetened pineapple juice

2 cups unsweetened fresh or frozen strawberries

2 medium-sized fresh or frozen bananas

¼ to ⅓ teaspoon **powdered stevia extract** (to taste)

• Place all the ingredients in a blender or food processor. Process until smooth. Frozen berries and frozen bananas will make the drink thick and creamy like a milk shake.

• To freeze bananas see page 181 under Frozen Fruit in Food Preparation Tips section.

VARIATION: *This is excellent made with a pineapple-coconut juice blend.*

Yield:
4 servings

Per serving:
Calories 173
Total Fat 1 g
Sat. Fat 0 g
Protein 2 g
Carb. 43 g
Fiber 3 g
Sodium 3 mg

✤ STRAWBERRY NOG

Smooth and cooling

2 cups unsweetened fresh or frozen strawberries

1½ cups soymilk or milk

1½ cups plain nonfat yogurt

½ to ¾ teaspoon **powdered stevia extract** (to taste)

1 teaspoon vanilla extract

2 ice cubes, crushed (optional)

• Process the strawberries, soymilk or milk, yogurt, stevia extract, and vanilla in a blender until smooth. Put the crushed ice in the blender with the rest of the ingredients, and blend until creamy.

• To crush the ice cubes, place them in a closed plastic bag, and hit them with a hammer.

Yield:
4 servings

Per serving:
Calories 95
Total Fat 2 g
Sat. Fat 1 g
Protein 9 g
Carb. 14 g
Fiber 2 g
Sodium 83 mg

❦ ORANGE COOLER

4 frozen, small to medium bananas

2 cups fresh or frozen orange juice (4 to 5 oranges)

1 cup plain nonfat yogurt

⅓ to ½ teaspoon **powdered stevia extract** (to taste)

4 to 6 ice cubes, crushed

• Cut up the bananas and process in a blender or food processor with the orange juice, yogurt, and stevia extract. Add the crushed ice and blend until creamy.

• To crush the ice cubes, place them in a closed plastic bag and hit with a hammer.

Yield:
4 servings

Per serving:
Calories 196
Total Fat 1 g
Sat. Fat 0 g
Protein 6 g
Carb. 44 g
Fiber 3 g
Sodium 50 mg

❦ MANGO PAPAYA SMOOTHIE

**This creamy treat is called
Mango Lassi in India.**

1 quart mango or papaya juice or a blend

1 cup plain nonfat yogurt

⅓ to ½ teaspoon **powdered stevia extract** (to taste)

• Mix the ingredients together in a blender until smooth.

NOTE: *This is an excellent beverage following a hot, spicy meal, especially Indian food.*

Yield:
4 servings
(large glasses)

Per serving:
Calories 165
Total Fat 0 g
Sat. Fat 0 g
Protein 4 g
Carb. 38 g
Fiber 0 g
Sodium 83 mg

# RASPBERRY CREAM

Suitable for a light dessert

2 cups unsweetened fresh or frozen raspberries

1 cup soymilk or milk

1 teaspoon vanilla

⅓ to ½ teaspoon **powdered stevia extract** (to taste)

1 (12.3-ounce) box silken tofu

2 tablespoons oil (optional)

• Combine the raspberries and soymilk or milk in a blender or food processor. Process until smooth. Add the vanilla, stevia extract, tofu, and oil. Blend until creamy. Place in dessert glasses and chill for 1 hour or more.

NOTE: *If you prefer, strain out the seeds by pouring through a fine-mesh strainer as you fill the serving glasses.*

OPTION: *To serve as a pudding dessert, use firm or extra-firm tofu.*

Yield:
4 servings

Per serving:
Calories 95
Total Fat 4 g
Sat. Fat 1 g
Protein 7 g
Carb. 10 g
Fiber 5 g
Sodium 13 mg

# CREAMY DATE SHAKE

Wonderfully thick and creamy—a real delight

4 large dates, pitted and chopped

1½ cups soymilk or milk

1 pound soft tofu

4 small to medium frozen bananas

2 teaspoons vanilla

¾ to 1 teaspoon **powdered stevia extract**

• Grind the chopped dates and part of the soymilk or milk together in a blender or food processor until the dates are well ground. Add the rest of the milk and the other ingredients, and blend until creamy. Use the pulse button at first, keeping the sides scraped down.

NOTE: *You may use a food processor. It's difficult to grind dates well in a blender. It helps to soften the chopped dates first in a little hot water for about 10 minutes. If you use the soak water in the shakes, cut back on the milk.*

VARIATION: *Use 1½ cups Vanilla Ice Cream (page 176) instead of tofu.*

Yield:
4 servings
(large glasses)

Per serving:
Calories 230
Total Fat 4 g
Sat. Fat 0 g
Protein 10 g
Carb. 42 g
Fiber 4 g
Sodium 55 mg

❀ ALMOND OR CASHEW MILK

1 cup raw almonds, blanched
or raw cashews

4 cups water

¼ to ⅓ teaspoon **powdered
stevia extract** (to taste)

2 tablespoons oil (optional)

Pinch of salt

Yield:
about 4 cups
(4 servings)

Per serving:
Calories 213
Total Fat 19 g
Sat. Fat 2 g
Protein 8 g
Carb. 7 g
Fiber 3 g
Sodium 4 mg

• To blanch the almonds, drop them into a pan of boiling water. Remove from the heat and let sit until the water cools. Slip off the skins with your thumb and index finger.

• Place either the blanched almonds or cashews in a blender with part of the water. Pulse on grind. Add the rest of the water, stevia extract, oil, and salt. Blend until smooth.

• Strain using a fine-mesh strainer. If cheesecloth is available, line the strainer with it. Press out the liquid. Pick up the cloth and squeeze. If you don't have cheesecloth, strain twice. Will store in the refrigerator for 4 to 5 days.

NOTE: *Use the pulp in baking, cooking, or as a bath scrub.*

❀ ALMOND MILKSHAKE

Yield:
about 4 cups
(4 servings)

3 cups almond milk

4 small to medium frozen bananas

1½ cups unsweetened, fresh or frozen strawberries, sliced

¼ to ⅓ teaspoon **powdered stevia extract** (to taste)

Per serving:
Calories 288
Total Fat 16 g
Sat. Fat 2 g
Protein 7 g
Carb. 36 g
Fiber 6 g
Sodium 5 mg

• Cut up the bananas and strawberries. Mix in a blender or food processor with the rest of the ingredients until creamy.

 Hot Carob "Cocoa"

Creamy and comforting

1 quart soymilk or milk
4 level tablespoons carob powder*
⅓ to ½ teaspoon **powdered stevia extract** (to taste)
Pinch of salt
1 teaspoon vanilla
2 tablespoons oil

• Combine the soymilk or milk, carob, stevia extract, salt, and vanilla in a blender on low. With the blender still running, slowly add the oil through the top of the blender.

• Pour into a pan and heat. Do not boil. Add more milk if this is too rich.

NOTE: *This beverage is rich and creamy made with almond or cashew milk. For a malt flavor, add a tablespoon of rice syrup or barley malt.*

Read about carob types on page 180 in Food Preparation Tips.

Yield:
4 servings

Per serving:
Calories 169
Total Fat 12 g
Sat. Fat 0 g
Protein 7 g
Carb. 10 g
Fiber 1 g
Sodium 56 mg

❈ Hot Cocoa

Rich and chocolaty—like Mom used to make

3 tablespoons cocoa

½ teaspoon **powdered stevia extract**

4 to 5 cups soymilk or milk

2 tablespoons honey or maple syrup

1 teaspoon vanilla extract

• Mix the cocoa and stevia extract together in a medium-sized saucepan. Add about ¼ cup of the soymilk or milk to the dry ingredients to make a paste. Gradually thin the paste with about ½ cup of the milk. Add the honey or maple syrup while bringing to a low boil. Boil for 2 to 3 minutes. Add the rest of the milk to the desired richness. Add the vanilla and return to burner until heated through.

NOTE: *Be careful not to scorch the cocoa. Use a pan with a heavy bottom and watch closely.*

VARIATION: *You may add a teaspoon of cinnamon and a pinch of nutmeg.*

Yield:
4 to 5 servings

Per serving:
Calories 120
Total Fat 5 g
Sat. Fat 0 g
Protein 8 g
Carb. 15 g
Fiber 1 g
Sodium 30 mg

Muffins and Breads

* For a nice full muffin, fill muffin tins to the top or even above the top. For really big muffins just fill 10 of the cups instead of 12.

* It may help to reduce sticking if you dust the muffin cups with flour after oiling.

* Twelve regular-sized muffins will make 24 mini-muffins. Baking times for mini-muffins will be 5 to 10 minutes less than for regular-sized muffins.

* If you don't have time to sift the flour with the other dry ingredients, at least mix all the dry ingredients together well in a bowl, and fluff the flour up with a fork.

* If the top of a quick bread is getting too dark, put foil over the top for the last 15 minutes of baking. If muffins are browning too quickly, reduce the oven temperature to 350°F for the last 15 minutes of baking.

* If your baking pans are dark or heavy or both, reduce oven temperature by 15 to 25°F.

* Muffin batter should stand up. It should not collapse when placed in the pan nor should it be as thick as quick bread.

* Be sure your leavenings are still active. To test baking powder see page 185.

* Do not over-mix quick breads.

* Cool the muffins in the pan for about 5 to 10 minutes before taking them out. Place on a rack.

* Replace 2 to 4 tablespoons of the wheat flour with soy flour in these quick bread recipes to make muffins and breads tender and give them a golden color. It also boosts the protein content.

CRANBERRY ORANGE MUFFINS

These are my favorite muffins. Serve during the holidays or anytime. Great with breakfast.

1 cup chopped fresh cranberries

¾ teaspoon **powdered stevia extract**

2 tablespoons honey or maple syrup, warmed (optional)

2¼ cups whole wheat pastry flour

¾ teaspoon baking soda

¾ teaspoon baking powder

¼ teaspoon salt

⅓ cup oil

1 large egg

2 tablespoons sesame tahini

⅓ cup plain nonfat yogurt

Grated rind of 1 orange

¾ cup fresh or frozen orange juice

• Preheat the oven to 375°F. Oil the muffin pans.

• Chop the cranberries by pulsing on grind in a blender or food processor a few times. Place in a small bowl. Mix the stevia extract and warmed honey or maple syrup into the cranberries. Set aside.

• Sift the flour, leavenings, and salt together in a bowl.

• In a large mixing bowl, beat the oil and egg together with a wire whisk. Mix in the tahini. Beat in the yogurt, then the orange rind and orange juice. Stir the sweetened cranberries into the batter.

• Fold the dry ingredients into the wet ingredients, stirring as little as possible. Spoon into the muffin pans. Bake 25 to 30 minutes. Remove from the pan and cool on a rack.

SUGGESTION: *Soak the cranberries in the stevia extract overnight on the counter or in the refrigerator.*

Yield:
12 muffins

Per muffin:
Calories 177
Total Fat 8 g
Sat. Fat 1 g
Protein 5 g
Carb. 20 g
Fiber 4 g
Sodium 158 mg

Yam Pecan Muffins

Great with soup or dinner.

1 packed cup cooked yams

½ teaspoon **powdered stevia extract**

¾ teaspoon **stevia concentrate**

2 tablespoons date sugar (optional)

½ teaspoon maple flavoring

1 tablespoon lemon juice

1 cup soymilk or milk

1¼ cups whole wheat pastry flour

1 cup unbleached white flour

1 teaspoon baking soda

1 teaspoon baking powder

1 teaspoon cinnamon

½ teaspoon nutmeg

¼ teaspoon salt

¾ cup chopped pecans

⅓ cup oil

2 large eggs

• Preheat the oven to 375°F. Oil the muffin tins.

• Cook the yams by peeling, cutting, and steaming in a covered pot. Measure out 1 cup of the packed yams, and place in a small bowl. Mix in the stevia extract, stevia concentrate, date sugar, and maple flavoring. Leave the yams a bit lumpy. Set aside to cool.

• In a cup, mix the lemon juice and soymilk or milk. Set aside. While the milk is curdling, sift the flours, leavenings, spices, and salt together in a bowl. Chop the pecans.

• Beat the oil and eggs together in a mixing bowl with a wire whisk. Beat in the soured milk. Stir in the sweetened yams.

• Stir the dry ingredients into the wet ingredients. Add the pecans just before the flour is completely mixed in. Save about ¼ cup of the pecans to sprinkle on the top. Press them in lightly. Spoon into the oiled muffin pans, and bake 25 to 30 minutes. Remove from the pan and cool on a rack.

Yield:
12 muffins

Per muffin:
Calories 218
Total Fat 12 g
Sat. Fat 1 g
Protein 6 g
Carb. 24 g
Fiber 3 g
Sodium 88 mg

⊠ Peanut Butter Banana Chocolate Chip Muffins

2 small to medium ripe bananas

½ cup unsweetened fruit juice (any type)

½ teaspoon **powdered stevia extract**

2 cups whole wheat pastry flour

½ teaspoon baking soda

½ teaspoon baking powder

¼ teaspoon salt (only if peanut butter is unsalted)

3 tablespoons oil

⅓ cup chunky or smooth natural peanut butter

1 large egg

½ cup plain nonfat yogurt or buttermilk

1 teaspoon vanilla extract

1 tablespoon lemon juice

⅓ cup chocolate or carob chips

• Preheat the oven to 375°F. Oil the muffin pans.

• Blend one of the bananas and the fruit juice together in a blender with the stevia extract. Set aside.

• Sift the flour, leavenings, and salt together in a bowl.

• Mix the oil and peanut butter together in a large mixing bowl. Beat in the egg. Stir in the yogurt or buttermilk and the vanilla. Mix the blended banana into the batter.

• Mash the other banana in a small bowl. Stir in the lemon juice. Gently stir the mashed bananas into the batter.

• Fold the dry ingredients into the wet, stirring as little as possible. Mix the chips in just before the flour is completely blended.

• Spoon into the muffin pans, and bake for 25 to 30 minutes. Remove from the pans and cool on a rack.

Yield:
12 muffins

Per muffin:
Calories 216
Total Fat 9 g
Sat. Fat 2 g
Protein 7 g
Carb. 26 g
Fiber 4 g
Sodium 102 mg

Blueberry Muffins

½ cup rolled oats
½ teaspoon **powdered stevia extract**
1 tablespoon date sugar (optional)
½ cup unsweetened pineapple juice
2 cups whole wheat pastry flour
¾ teaspoon baking soda
1 teaspoon baking powder
¼ teaspoon salt
⅓ cup oil
1 large egg
⅓ cup plain nonfat yogurt
½ cup soymilk or milk
2 tablespoons orange juice concentrate
1 teaspoon vanilla extract
1 cup fresh or frozen blueberries

• Preheat the oven to 375°F. Thaw the blueberries if frozen. Oil the muffin pans.

• Soak the oats, stevia extract, and date sugar in the pineapple juice for 10 to 15 minutes in a small bowl. (Note: If using quick oats don't soak them in the pineapple juice; they get too soggy. Add with the other dry ingredients.)

• Sift the flour, leavenings, and salt together in a bowl.

• Beat the oil and egg together in a mixing bowl. Thin the yogurt with the soymilk or milk and add to the other liquid ingredients. Stir in the orange juice concentrate, vanilla, and soaked oats. Mix in the blueberries.

• Fold the dry ingredients into the wet ingredients, stirring as little as possible.

• Spoon the batter into the muffin pans, and bake for 25 to 30 minutes. Remove from the pans and cool on a rack.

Yield:
12 muffins

Per muffin:
Calories 177
Total Fat 7 g
Sat. Fat 1 g
Protein 5 g
Carb. 22 g
Fiber 3 g
Sodium 166 mg

✿ SQUASH CORN MUFFINS

1½ cups cooked squash (packed)

½ teaspoon **powdered stevia extract**

½ teaspoon **stevia concentrate** or
   1 tablespoon molasses

1¾ cups soymilk or milk

2 tablespoons lemon juice

½ cup oil

2 large eggs

2 cups whole wheat pastry flour

1½ cups corn flour

1½ teaspoons baking soda

2 teaspoons baking powder

1 teaspoon cinnamon

½ teaspoon salt

• Preheat the oven to 350°F. Oil the muffin pans.

• Steam or bake the squash. Measure the squash and place in
a small bowl. Stir in the stevia extract and stevia concentrate
or molasses. Set aside.

• Mix the soymilk or milk and lemon juice. Set aside to sour.

• Whip together the oil and eggs. Stir in the soured milk. Fold
in the squash, just lightly mixing.

• Sift together the flours, leavenings, cinnamon, and salt. Fold
the dry ingredients into the wet without over-mixing.

• Spoon into the muffin pans, and bake for 25 to 30 minutes.
Remove from pans and cool on a rack.

NOTE: *Sweet squash, like butternut or delicata, works best.*

OPTION: *Add ½ cup fresh or frozen corn, thawed.*

Yield:
16 muffins

Per muffin:
Calories 191
Total Fat 9 g
Sat. Fat 1 g
Protein 5 g
Carb. 23 g
Fiber 3 g
Sodium 244 mg

APPLE BRAN MUFFINS

¼ cup chopped dried figs or raisins

⅓ cup unsweetened apple juice or water

½ teaspoon **powdered stevia extract**

3 tablespoons oil

1 large egg

½ teaspoon maple flavoring

Grated rind of ½ orange

½ cup plain nonfat yogurt or 4 ounces soft tofu

¼ cup unsweetened apple butter

¼ cup fresh or frozen orange juice

1¼ cups whole wheat flour

¾ cup wheat or oat bran

1 teaspoon baking soda

1 teaspoon baking powder

¼ teaspoon salt

¼ teaspoon nutmeg

½ cup chopped apples

¼ cup chopped nuts or sunflower seeds

• Preheat the oven to 350°F. Oil the muffin pans.

• Simmer the figs or raisins in the apple juice or water and stevia extract for 10 to 15 minutes until softened.

• Beat the oil and egg together in a mixing bowl. Add the maple flavoring and orange rind. Mix in the yogurt, apple butter, and orange juice. (If using tofu, blend the tofu with the apple butter and the orange juice in a blender first.) Mix in the stewed fruit.

• Mix the flour, bran, leavenings, salt, and nutmeg together in a bowl. Fold the dry ingredients into the wet, stirring as little as possible. Fold in the chopped apples and nuts before the flour is completely blended.

• Spoon the batter into the muffin pans, and bake for 25 to 30 minutes. Remove from pans and cool on a rack.

Yield:
12 muffins

Per muffin:
Calories 139
Total Fat 6 g
Sat. Fat 1 g
Protein 4 g
Carb. 19 g
Fiber 4 g
Sodium 194 mg

✳ PEACH MUFFINS

½ cup soymilk or milk

1 tablespoon lemon juice

2 cups whole wheat pastry flour

½ teaspoon baking soda

1 teaspoon baking powder

¼ teaspoon salt

½ cup oat bran

1½ cups chopped peaches, fresh or frozen, thawed, or one 15-ounce can, drained

¼ cup oil

1 large egg

½ teaspoon **powdered stevia extract**

1 teaspoon vanilla extract

1 tablespoon frozen orange juice concentrate

1 teaspoon grated fresh ginger or ¾ teaspoon dried powdered ginger

• Preheat the oven to 375°F. Oil the muffin pans.

• Mix the soymilk or milk and lemon juice in a cup. Set aside to sour.

• Sift the flour, leavenings, and salt together in a large mixing bowl. If using dried ginger, sift it in with the other dry ingredients. Stir in the oat bran.

• Blend 1 cup of the chopped peaches, the soured milk, oil, egg, stevia extract, vanilla, and orange juice concentrate in a blender until smooth.

• Make a well in the dry ingredients, and fold in the wet ingredients quickly and gently. Add the remaining chopped peaches and fresh ginger just before the flour is completely blended.

• Spoon the batter into the muffin pans, and bake for 30 to 35 minutes. Remove from the pans and cool on a rack.

Yield:
12 muffins

Per muffin:
Calories 151
Total Fat 6 g
Sat. Fat 1 g
Protein 5 g
Carb. 21 g
Fiber 4 g
Sodium 134 mg

 ZUCCHINI MUFFINS

1 lightly packed cup grated zucchini

⅓ teaspoon **powdered stevia extract**

2 tablespoons honey, warmed

1¾ cups whole wheat pastry flour

¼ cup soy flour

1 teaspoon baking soda

1 teaspoon baking powder

1 teaspoon **powdered stevia herb**

1 teaspoon cinnamon

½ teaspoon nutmeg

¼ teaspoon salt

⅓ cup oil

1 egg

½ cup unsweetened applesauce

½ cup plain nonfat yogurt or buttermilk

1 teaspoon vanilla extract

½ teaspoon **stevia concentrate**

⅓ cup chopped walnuts or sunflower seeds (optional)

- Preheat the oven to 375°F. Oil the muffin pans.

- Grate the zucchini and measure it out, lightly packing the cup. After measuring, squeeze the water out of the zucchini by using a cheesecloth or by squeezing with your hands. Warm the honey in a microwave oven. Place the pressed zucchini in a small bowl, and mix in the stevia extract and honey. Set aside.

- Sift the flours, leavenings, stevia herb, spices, and salt together in a bowl.

- In a mixing bowl beat the oil and egg together with a wire whisk. Beat in the applesauce, yogurt or buttermilk, vanilla, and stevia concentrate, and mix well. Stir in the sweetened, grated zucchini.

- Fold the dry ingredients into the wet ingredients, stirring quickly. Add the nuts or sunflower seeds just before the batter is completely blended. Spoon into muffin pans.

- Bake for 25 to 30 minutes. Remove from the pans and cool on a rack.

Yield:

Per muffin:
Calories 159
Total Fat 7 g
Sat. Fat 1 g
Protein 5 g
Carb. 19 g
Fiber 3 g
Sodium 149 mg

CARROT MUFFINS

½ cup unsweetened applesauce

1 tablespoon date sugar (optional)

⅓ teaspoon **powdered stevia extract**

1 lightly packed cup grated carrots

2 cups whole wheat pastry flour

¾ teaspoon baking soda

1 teaspoon baking powder

1 teaspoon **powdered stevia herb**

¾ teaspoon cinnamon

¼ teaspoon nutmeg

¼ teaspoon salt

⅓ cup oil

1 egg

¼ cup plain nonfat yogurt

1 teaspoon vanilla

½ cup unsweetened pineapple juice
   or pineapple juice blend

½ teaspoon **stevia concentrate**

⅓ cup chopped walnuts

¼ cup raisins (optional)

• Preheat the oven to 375°F. Oil the muffin pans.

• Warm the applesauce in a small bowl or cup in a microwave. Mix in the date sugar and stevia extract. Set aside. Grate the carrots.

• Sift the flour, leavenings, stevia herb, spices, and salt together in a bowl.

• In a large mixing bowl, beat the oil and egg together, and mix in the yogurt. Add the sweetened applesauce, vanilla, pineapple juice, and stevia concentrate. Stir in the carrots. Mix well.

• Stir the dry ingredients into the wet. Add the nuts and raisins just before flour is completely mixed.

• Spoon into the muffin pans and bake for 25 to 30 minutes. Remove from pans and cool on a rack.

Yield:
12 muffins

Per muffin:
Calories 175
Total Fat 9 g
Sat. Fat 1 g
Protein 5 g
Carb. 19 g
Fiber 3 g
Sodium 166 mg

DATE NUT BREAD

4 large dates, chopped

¼ cup apple juice or water

½ teaspoon **powdered stevia extract**

2¼ cups whole wheat pastry flour

½ teaspoon baking soda

1 teaspoon baking powder

¼ teaspoon salt

⅓ cup oil

2 eggs

¾ cup unsweetened applesauce

¼ cup plain nonfat yogurt

½ teaspoon **stevia concentrate**

1 teaspoon vanilla

½ cup chopped walnuts

- Preheat the oven to 350°F. Oil a medium-sized loaf pan.
- Chop the dates into a small pan. Add the apple juice or water and the stevia extract. Soften the dates over low heat for 2 to 3 minutes. Set aside.
- Sift the flour, leavenings, and salt together in a bowl.
- Beat the oil and eggs together in a large mixing bowl. Mix in the applesauce, yogurt, stevia concentrate, and vanilla. Mix in the softened dates.
- Mix the dry ingredients into the wet, stirring just enough to mix. Add the nuts just before the flour is completely mixed in.
- Spoon the batter into the loaf pan, and bake for 55 to 60 minutes. Turn out the loaf and cool on a rack.

Yield:
12 servings

Per serving:
Calories 206
Total Fat 11 g
Sat. Fat 1 g
Protein 6 g
Carb. 22 g
Fiber 4 g
Sodium 143 mg

APPLESAUCE GINGERBREAD

1¾ cups whole wheat pastry flour

½ teaspoon baking soda

¾ teaspoon baking powder

1 teaspoon powdered ginger

½ teaspoon cinnamon

¼ teaspoon allspice

¼ teaspoon nutmeg

¼ teaspoon salt

⅓ cup oil

1 large egg

¼ cup plain nonfat yogurt

2 tablespoons date sugar (optional)

½ teaspoon **powdered stevia extract**

½ teaspoon vanilla extract

½ teaspoon maple flavoring

1 cup unsweetened applesauce

⅓ cup chopped sunflower seeds (optional)

Yield:
16 servings

Per serving:
Calories 104
Total Fat 5 g
Sat. Fat 0 g
Protein 3 g
Carb. 11 g
Fiber 2 g
Sodium 97 mg

• Preheat the oven to 350°F. Oil an 8-inch, shallow, square pan.

• Sift the flour, leavenings, spices, and salt together in a bowl.

• Whip the oil and egg together in a mixing bowl, and mix in the yogurt. Stir in the date sugar, stevia extract, vanilla, and maple flavoring. Mix in the applesauce and beat until smooth.

• Fold the dry ingredients into the wet ingredients. Add sunflower seeds, if desired. Minimize the stirring.

• Spoon the batter into the pan, and smooth the top. Bake for 30 to 35 minutes.

• Serve warm, topped with whipped cream or ice cream.

NOTE: *A little more or less flour may be needed depending on how thick the applesauce is to start with.*

BANANA BREAD

2 very ripe, medium to large bananas

¼ teaspoon **powdered stevia extract**

½ teaspoon **stevia concentrate**

1 tablespoon lemon juice

2 cups whole wheat pastry flour

½ teaspoon baking soda

1 teaspoon baking powder

¼ teaspoon salt

⅓ cup oil

1 large egg

½ cup plain nonfat yogurt or buttermilk

1 teaspoon vanilla extract

½ cup chopped walnuts (optional)

• Preheat the oven to 350°F. Oil a medium-sized loaf pan (7½ x 3½ x 2½ inches).

• Mash the bananas in a small bowl. Mix the stevia extract, stevia concentrate, and lemon juice into the mashed bananas. Set aside.

• Sift the flour, leavenings, and salt together in a bowl.

• Beat the oil and egg together in a mixing bowl until creamy. Beat in the yogurt or buttermilk and the vanilla. Stir the mashed bananas into the liquid mixture.

• Fold the dry ingredients into the wet ingredients, stirring as little as possible. Mix in the walnuts just before the flour is completely blended.

• Place into the loaf pan. Bake for 50 minutes to 1 hour until a toothpick or fork stuck in the middle comes out clean. Turn out the loaf and cool on a rack.

NOTE: *For maximum flavor, use very ripe bananas (brown-spotted).*

Yield:
12 servings

Per serving:
Calories 162
Total Fat 7 g
Sat. Fat 1 g
Protein 5 g
Carb. 20 g
Fiber 3 g
Sodium 141 mg

✤ BREAKFAST SWEET ROLLS

These rolls are easy to make and very good.

BREAD MACHINE DOUGH

1 cup water

1 large egg

3 tablespoons oil

1½ tablespoons honey*

½ teaspoon salt

1 tablespoon **powdered stevia leaf**

3 cups whole wheat bread flour

1 package dry yeast

• Mix the stevia leaf into the flour first. Add the ingredients to the bread machine pan in the order listed. Set the machine to the Dough Cycle, and start the machine.

• Remove the dough to a lightly floured board. Roll it out into a rectangle approximately 10 x 18 inches about ¼ inch thick.

*A small amount of sugar is necessary for the yeast to grow.

FILLING

1 cup coarsely ground walnuts

½ teaspoon **powdered stevia extract**

½ teaspoon **stevia concentrate**

1 teaspoon cinnamon

6 dates, chopped

⅔ cup water

1 teaspoon vanilla

• While the dough is in the machine, prepare the filling. Chop the walnuts and mix in a small bowl with the stevia extract, stevia concentrate, and cinnamon. Set aside.

• Preheat the oven to 350°F.

• Cut up the dates and place them in a small pan. Cover with the water and cook to a creamy paste. Stir in the vanilla. Spread the paste over the rolled-out dough. Sprinkle the nut mixture evenly over the date paste.

• Start at one long edge and roll up the dough. Cut into 1-inch sections, and place on a buttered cookie sheet. Flatten the rolls with the palm of your hand. Cover with a cloth and let rise in a warm location for 45 minutes to 1 hour.

• Bake for 25 to 30 minutes. Butter the tops upon removal from oven.

Yield:
18 rolls

Per roll:
Calories 149
Total Fat 7 g
Sat. Fat 1 g
Protein 4 g
Carb. 19 g
Fiber 3 g
Sodium 65 mg

✳ Yam Drop Biscuits

½ packed cup cooked yams

1½ cups whole wheat pastry flour

¼ teaspoon salt

¼ teaspoon **powdered stevia extract** AND/OR
   1 teaspoon **powdered stevia leaf**

3 tablespoons butter or margarine

½ cup soymilk or milk

- Preheat the oven to 400°F.

- Cook the yam by peeling, cutting into pieces, and steaming.

- Sift the flour, salt, stevia extract, and powdered stevia leaf (optional) together into a large mixing bowl. Cut the butter or margarine into the flour with a pastry blender or fork until evenly distributed.

- Blend the soymilk or milk and yam together in the blender. Make a well in the center of the flour. Pour the liquid into the flour, and mix. The batter should pull away from the sides of the bowl. Add a little more flour if necessary.

- Drop from a spoon onto an unoiled cookie sheet. Bake for 12 to 15 minutes.

NOTE: *You may use 3 tablespoons of oil instead of butter or margarine, but the flavor and texture will not be as good. Also be careful about adding too much flour.*

Yield:
16 biscuits

Per biscuit:
Calories 74
Total Fat 3 g
Sat. Fat 2 g
Protein 2 g
Carb. 10 g
Fiber 2 g
Sodium 61 mg

Cakes

* For a finer texture, sift the flour and leavenings twice. I sift twice using a triple sifter and it takes no time at all.

* Cakes can be troublesome; forming surface cracks, puffing up in the center, or collapsing after being taken out of the oven. Know your oven and baking pans. If your pans are dark and/or heavy, reduce the oven temperature by 25°F or more. You may have to double the pan if your pans are very thin. Try placing cakes in the lower third of the oven. Try to buy medium-weight cake pans that are shiny on the outside.

* Butter or oil and flour the pans—even nonstick pans. A thin even film of fat with a fine dusting of flour is good.

* For cakes, have all the ingredients at room temperature, about 70°F.

* Fill cake pans from about ½ to ⅔ full. If the batter is too skimpy in the pan, it won't rise as well. If the pan is too full, the cake may sink after taking it out of the oven. If you don't have the exact size pan called for in the recipe, use the closest size available.

* To keep the cake from peaking in the center, smooth the surface of the cake with a spatula, or even have the batter in the center be a little lower than the sides. For a layer cake, the peak can be sliced off.

* In general, the beating of cake batter should be done before the flour is added. The eggs and other liquid ingredients can be beaten until light and fluffy. Once the flour is added just stir until the batter is well mixed and smooth.

* Use guar gum, or some other gum, in cakes without eggs. Guar gum helps the ingredients bind together and the cake rise better.

* Cake can be stored for a day or two on the counter in a container with air flow (in a covered cake dish or covered with foil) unless it has a frosting or filling that needs refrigeration.

* Refrigerated or frozen servings of cake become light and tender when warmed in a microwave oven for about 25 to 35 seconds.

# CHEESECAKE

CRUMB CRUST (single 9-inch)

1½ cups graham cracker or gingersnap crumbs

2 to 3 tablespoons butter or margarine, melted

2 to 3 tablespoons fruit juice

• Preheat the oven to 300°F.

• Place the crackers or cookies in a plastic bag, close the bag, and crush with a rolling pin. Place in a small bowl.

• Melt the butter or margarine, and mix it into the crumbs a little at a time with a fork until well distributed. (It will look like slightly wet coarse sand.) Sprinkle in the fruit juice, and stir until evenly mixed. Mix in just enough juice to make the grains start clumping together. Press the crumbs into the bottom of an 8 or 9-inch springform pan and 1 inch up the side, using your fingers or a fork. Bake in a 300°F oven for 15 minutes. Cool.

• (*Note:* Omit the following procedure for making the filling if using a food processor. Simply put all the filling ingredients together in the processor container, and mix well.)

FILLING

4 cups low-fat cottage cheese

2 tablespoons butter or margarine, melted

4 eggs

¼ cup maple syrup or honey

1 teaspoon **powdered stevia extract**

1 teaspoon vanilla extract

¼ teaspoon salt

¼ cup wheat flour

Juice of one lemon
   (3 tablespoons)

Grated rind of one lemon

- If mixing by hand, proceed with the following directions. Press the cottage cheese through a fine-mesh strainer. Blend the melted butter into the cottage cheese.

- Beat the eggs in a small bowl, and add in 4 parts to the cottage cheese, beating well after each addition. Mix in the maple syrup or honey, stevia extract, vanilla, salt, flour, lemon juice, and lemon rind. Stir until the mixture is smooth and thoroughly blended.

- Pour the batter gently into the cake pan. Bake for 1 hour. Shut the oven off but leave the cake inside the oven for 1½ more hours. Do not open the oven door.

- Chill the cake in the refrigerator before serving. Up to 12 hours is recommended.

- Top with Strawberry Topping (optional) before serving.

Yield:
10 servings

Per serving:
Calories 239
Total Fat 10 g
Sat. Fat 5 g
Protein 15 g
Carb. 22 g
Fiber .6 g
Sodium 601 mg

optional Strawberry Topping on next page

🌸 STRAWBERRY TOPPING FOR CHEESECAKE

2 cups fresh strawberries

¼ cup water

1 teaspoon honey

⅛ teaspoon **powdered stevia extract**

1 tablespoon cornstarch or arrowroot powder

• Slice 1½ cups of the berries in half lengthwise and arrange over the top of the cheesecake.

• Crush the other ½ cup of berries, and place in a small saucepan with the ¼ cup of water. Simmer for about 3 minutes, and strain out the pulp.

• Return the strawberry juice to the pan. Mix in the honey, stevia extract, and cornstarch. Cook on low until it thickens.

• Pour the glaze over the strawberries on top of the cheesecake.

Yield:
10 servings

Per serving:
Calories 14
Total Fat 0 g
Sat. Fat 0 g
Protein 0 g
Carb. 3 g
Fiber .7 g
Sodium 0 mg

MAPLE TOFU CHEESECAKE

CRUST

See crust recipe page 58. Use an 8 or
9-inch springform pan.

FILLING

2 pounds firm tofu, drained

⅓ cup oil

1 teaspoon **powdered stevia extract**

¼ cup maple syrup

2 tablespoons apple butter

½ teaspoon maple flavoring

1 teaspoon vanilla extract

⅛ teaspoon salt

• Preheat the oven to 300°F.

• While the crust is in the oven, drain the tofu on paper towels. You can hasten this process by placing a plate on top for about 10 to 15 minutes.

• Raise oven temperature to 325°F.

• Process all the ingredients together in a food processor or blender until creamy. If using a blender, it will have to be done in two batches. Use the pulse button until it is smooth enough to blend.

• Spoon the filling into the crust. Place a tray or cookie sheet on the lower rack beneath the pan for leakage. Bake for 45 to 50 minutes. (Note: If the top surface of the cheesecake cracks, reduce the oven temperature 15°F to 25°F, or turn off the oven if baking time is nearly over.) Turn off the oven but leave the pan in for ½ hour longer. Cool on the counter, then refrigerate 6 hours or more before serving.

Yield:
10 servings

Per serving:
Calories 312
Total Fat 19 g
Sat. Fat 4 g
Protein 15 g
Carb. 23 g
Fiber 2 g
Sodium 170 mg

CHOCOLATE TOFU CHEESECAKE

CRUST

See crust recipe page 58. Use an 8 or 9-inch springform pan.

FILLING

2 cups chocolate chips (malt sweetened, regular semi-sweet, or
    carob chips)
2 pounds firm tofu, drained
¼ cup oil
1 teaspoon **powdered stevia extract**
1 teaspoon vanilla extract
⅛ teaspoon salt

• Preheat the oven to 300°F.

• While the crust is in the oven, drain the tofu on paper towels. You can hasten the process by placing a plate on top for about 10 to 15 minutes.

• Raise oven temperature to 325°F.

• Melt the chocolate chips over low heat in a small heavy-bottomed pan. Stir in the oil and stevia extract.

• Place the tofu and other filling ingredients in the container of a food processor or blender. Add the melted chocolate.

- Process all the ingredients together until creamy. If you are using a blender, it will have to be done in two batches. Use the pulse button until it is smooth enough to blend.

- Spoon the filling into the crust. Place a tray or cookie sheet on lower rack beneath the pan for leakage. Bake for 45 to 50 minutes. (Note: If the top surface of the cheesecake cracks, reduce the oven temperature 15°F to 25°F, or turn off the oven if the baking time is nearly over.) Turn off the oven but leave the pan in for ½ hour longer. Cool on the counter, then refrigerate 6 hours or more before serving.

Yield:
10 servings

Per serving:
Calories 447
Total Fat 17 g
Sat. Fat 10 g
Protein 17 g
Carb. 36 g
Fiber 3 g
Sodium 169 mg

CHOCOLATE CHEESECAKE

CRUST

See crust recipe page 58. Use an 8- or 9-inch springform pan.

FILLING

4 squares baker's chocolate

2 tablespoons butter

4 cups low-fat cottage cheese

4 eggs

⅓ cup honey or maple syrup

1 teaspoon **powdered stevia extract**

1 teaspoon vanilla extract

¼ teaspoon salt

¼ cup flour

• Preheat the oven to 300°F.

• Melt the baker's chocolate over low heat in a small, heavy-bottomed pan. Add the butter and melt.

• (Note: Omit the following procedure for making the filling if using a food processor. Simply put all the filling ingredients and the melted chocolate/butter together in the processor container, and mix well. If mixing by hand, proceed with the following directions.)

• Press the cottage cheese through a fine-mesh strainer. Place in a mixing bowl, and add the melted chocolate and butter.

• Beat the eggs in a small bowl, and add in 4 parts to the cottage cheese, beating well after each addition. Mix in the honey or maple syrup, stevia extract, vanilla, salt, and flour. Stir until the mixture is smooth and thoroughly blended.

• Pour gently into the crust. Bake for 1 hour. Shut the oven off but leave the cake inside for 1½ hours longer. Do not open the oven door.

• Cool on the counter, then chill the cake in the refrigerator before serving. Up to 12 hours or more is recommended.

Yield:
10 servings

Per serving:
Calories 308
Total Fat 16 g
Sat. Fat 9 g
Protein 16 g
Carb. 28 g
Fiber 2 g
Sodium 603 mg

 # SPICE CAKE

⅓ cup oil

½ cup unsweetened applesauce

1 teaspoon **stevia concentrate**

¼ teaspoon **stevia extract**

1 tablespoon molasses (optional)

2 eggs

⅓ cup plain nonfat yogurt

⅓ cup soymilk or milk

1 cup whole wheat pastry flour

¾ cup unbleached white flour

½ teaspoon baking soda

1 teaspoon baking powder

1¼ teaspoons cinnamon

½ teaspoon nutmeg

¼ teaspoon cloves

¼ teaspoon salt

• Preheat the oven to 350°F. Oil and flour an 8-inch square or 9-inch round cake pan.

• Beat the oil, applesauce, stevia concentrate, stevia extract, and molasses together in a mixing bowl. Beat in the eggs one at a time until the batter is fluffy. Thin the yogurt with the soymilk or milk, and beat into the other liquid ingredients.

• Sift the flours, leavenings, spices, and salt together twice. Stir the dry ingredients into the wet ingredients until they are well blended.

• Spoon the batter into the pan. Smooth the top with a spatula, and bake for 35 to 40 minutes.

SERVING SUGGESTION: *Top with Cream Cheese Frosting (page 162) or Lemon Icing (page 161).*

Yield:
12 servings

Per serving:
Calories 140
Total Fat 7 g
Sat. Fat 1 g
Protein 4 g
Carb. 15 g
Fiber 2 g
Sodium 143 mg

DUTCH APPLE CAKE

TOPPING

2 cups chopped apples (about 2 large apples)

½ cup chopped almonds or walnuts

2 large dates, chopped

¾ teaspoon cinnamon

¼ teaspoon nutmeg

½ teaspoon almond or vanilla extract

Pinch of salt

⅓ teaspoon **powdered stevia extract**

½ teaspoon **stevia concentrate**

1 tablespoon lemon juice

• Preheat the oven to 350°F. Butter a medium-sized casserole dish or glass baking pan (about 8-inch round).

• Chop the apples into thin pieces, and place in a mixing bowl. Chop the nuts and dates, and mix with the apples. Stir all the rest of the topping ingredients into the apples. Place in the bottom of the baking pan.

CAKE

2 cups whole wheat pastry flour

1 teaspoon baking soda

¼ teaspoon salt

½ teaspoon **powdered stevia extract**

¼ cup butter

1 egg

1 cup buttermilk

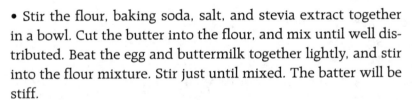

Yield:
8 servings

Per serving:
Calories 283
Total Fat 13 g
Sat. Fat 5 g
Protein 9 g
Carb. 34 g
Fiber 6 g
Sodium 340 mg

• Stir the flour, baking soda, salt, and stevia extract together in a bowl. Cut the butter into the flour, and mix until well distributed. Beat the egg and buttermilk together lightly, and stir into the flour mixture. Stir just until mixed. The batter will be stiff.

• Spoon the batter over the apples. Bake for 40 to 45 minutes. Upon removal from the oven, loosen the sides of the cake and immediately turn over onto a plate.

Carob Pecan Cake

½ cup butter, softened

2 tablespoons date sugar (optional)

¾ teaspoon **powdered stevia extract**

¾ cup carob powder*

3 eggs, warmed to room temperature

½ cup soymilk or milk

½ cup plain nonfat yogurt

½ cup unsweetened applesauce

1½ teaspoons vanilla extract

2 cups whole wheat pastry flour

1 teaspoon baking soda

1½ teaspoons baking powder

¼ teaspoon salt

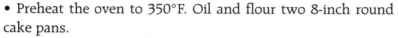

Yield:
10 servings

Per serving:
Calories 256
Total Fat 12 g
Sat. Fat 7 g
Protein 7 g
Carb. 29 g
Fiber 5 g
Sodium 363 mg

• Preheat the oven to 350°F. Oil and flour two 8-inch round cake pans.

• Soften and cream the butter in a mixing bowl. Cream in the date sugar, stevia extract, and about ¼ cup of the carob powder. Beat in the eggs with a hand mixer. Add the rest of the carob, and beat. Mix in the soymilk or milk, yogurt, applesauce, and vanilla.

• Sift the dry ingredients together. Add the dry ingredients to the wet ingredients, mixing just until well blended. Spoon into the pans, and smooth the top. Bake for 22 to 25 minutes. Cool 5 minutes in the pans, then turn out onto a rack.

❁ CAROB DATE FROSTING

8 to 10 dates, chopped

⅓ to ½ cup unsweetened fruit juice

⅔ cup carob powder

⅔ cup water

2 tablespoons butter

⅓ teaspoon **powdered stevia extract**

1 teaspoon vanilla extract

½ cup coarsely ground pecans

• In a small saucepan, cook the dates in the fruit juice, stirring occasionally until smooth and creamy. If the dates won't completely cream, push them through a strainer. Set aside.

• In another small pan, cook the carob powder and water at a low boil for 5 to 8 minutes. Beat in the butter, stevia extract, and vanilla. Add the cooked dates and beat until well blended.

• Spread some of the frosting between the cake layers. Spread the rest of the frosting on the top and sides of the cake. Grind the pecans in the blender. Sprinkle the nuts on the top of the cake.

Read about types of carob in Food Preparation Tips on page 180.

Yield:
(10 servings)

Per serving:
Calories 94
Total Fat 4 g
Sat. Fat 2 g
Protein 1 g
Carb. 14 g
Fiber 2 g
Sodium 26 mg

✿ STRAWBERRY CREAM CAKE

DOUBLE-LAYER BUTTER CAKE

½ cup butter, softened

3 tablespoons honey, warmed

1 teaspoon **stevia extract**

3 eggs, warmed to room temperature

¼ cup non-instant dry milk powder

½ cup plain nonfat yogurt

¾ cup water

1 teaspoon vanilla extract

1 cup whole wheat pastry flour

1 cup unbleached flour

1 teaspoon baking soda

1 teaspoon baking powder

¼ teaspoon salt

• Place a rack in the lower third of the oven. Preheat the oven to 350°F. Oil and flour two 8-inch round cake pans.

• Cream the softened butter with a mixer or wire whisk in a large mixing bowl. Beat in the honey and stevia extract until light and fluffy. Beat in the eggs one at a time. Mix in the milk powder.

• Mix the yogurt, water, and vanilla together in a cup or small bowl.

• Sift the flours, leavenings, and salt together twice. Mix a third of the flour into the butter batter. Stir in half of the yogurt-water mixture. Mix in another third of the flour, then the other half of the liquid, and finally the last of the flour. Work quickly and don't over-beat. Mix just until well blended.

• Divide the batter between the two pans. Smooth the top surfaces with a spatula. Bake for 30 to 35 minutes or until a toothpick inserted in the center comes out clean. Cool in the pans for 10 minutes. Turn the cakes onto a cooling rack.

• If the center of the cakes peak, shave off at least one of the layers so it is flat.

✿ FILLING AND TOPPING

⅔ cup Strawberry Filling (page 159)
2 cups fresh strawberries
Whipped cream

• Lay sliced fresh strawberries on the top of the bottom layer. Put a generous layer of Strawberry Filling on top of the berries. Place the second layer on top of the bottom. Serve the cake topped with whipped cream and whole berries, or frost with Lemon Icing (page 161) or Coconut Frosting (page 163).

Yield:
10 servings

Per serving:
(includes topping)
Calories 268
Total Fat 14 g
Sat. Fat 14 g
Protein 8 g
Carb. 34 g
Fiber 3 g
Sodium 336 mg

BLUEBERRY TOFU BUNDT CAKE

⅔ cup oil

½ (12.3-ounce) box silken tofu (drained)

1 tablespoon sesame tahini or almond butter

1 teaspoon **powdered stevia extract**

2 tablespoons date sugar

2 tablespoons maple syrup

½ teaspoon maple flavoring

1 teaspoon vanilla extract

¼ cup lemon juice

¾ cup unsweetened applesauce

½ cup soymilk or milk

1¾ cups whole wheat pastry flour

1 cup unbleached white flour

1 teaspoon baking soda

2 teaspoons baking powder

1 teaspoon guar gum

¼ teaspoon cardamom

½ teaspoon salt

⅔ cup fresh or frozen, thawed blueberries

- Preheat the oven to 350°F. Oil and dust with flour a 10 to 12-cup bundt pan. Place a rack in the lower third of the oven.

- Mix the oil, tofu, tahini or almond butter, stevia extract, date sugar, maple syrup, maple flavoring, vanilla, lemon juice, applesauce, and soymilk or milk together in a blender until smooth.

- Sift the flours, leavenings, guar gum, cardamom, and salt together twice, and place in a large mixing bowl. Make a well in the dry ingredients, and pour in the blender mixture. Beat until well mixed (15 to 20 strokes). Stir in the blueberries.

- Spoon the batter into the pan and smooth the top with a spatula. Bake for 55 to 65 minutes or until a toothpick inserted in the cake comes out clean. Cover the pan with foil for the last 15 minutes if the top is getting too brown. Cool in the pan for 10 minutes, then turn onto a cooling rack. Top generously with warm Berry Sauce (page 156) or Lemon Icing (page 161). Let the sauce or icing run down the sides of the cake.

Yield:
12 servings

Per serving:
Calories 253
Total Fat 13 g
Sat. Fat 1 g
Protein 5 g
Carb. 29 g
Fiber 3 g
Sodium 258 mg

✿ LEMON POPPYSEED CAKE

½ cup poppyseeds

1 cup soymilk or milk

½ cup oil

2 tablespoons sesame tahini or almond butter

3 tablespoons maple syrup or honey

1 teaspoon **powdered stevia extract**

1 teaspoon vanilla or almond extract

½ cup unsweetened applesauce

¼ cup lemon juice

Grated rind of 1 lemon

3 eggs

1½ cups whole wheat pastry flour

1 cup unbleached white flour

1 teaspoon baking soda

1½ teaspoons baking powder

½ teaspoon salt

• Preheat the oven to 350°F. Oil and dust with flour a 10 or 12 cup bundt pan. Place a rack in the lower third of the oven.

Yield:
12 servings

Per serving:
Calories 264
Total Fat 15 g
Sat. Fat 2 g
Protein 7 g
Carb. 25 g
Fiber 4 g
Sodium 261 mg

• Grind the poppyseeds in a blender; pulse 3 or 4 times only. Heat the soymilk or milk to the boiling point in a small pan. Turn off the heat and mix in the poppyseeds. Set aside.

• Mix the oil and tahini or almond butter together in a large bowl. Beat in the honey or maple syrup and stevia extract. Add the vanilla or almond extract, applesauce, lemon juice, and lemon rind. Beat the eggs well in a small bowl. Add the eggs to the batter, and beat with a hand mixer until the batter is fluffy.

• Sift the flours, leavenings, and salt together twice. Alternate adding the flour and milk/poppyseeds to the egg batter. Mix in a third of the flour, then ½ of the milk, ⅓ of the flour, the other half of the milk, and finally the rest of the flour. Work quickly and do not over-mix. Spoon into the pan. Smooth the top with a spatula. Bake for 40 to 45 minutes. Cool in the pan for 5 to 10 minutes, then turn onto a rack.

• Top with Lemon Icing (page 161) or use Cream Cheese Frosting (page 162). If using Lemon Icing, frost when the cake is still hot, and let the icing run down the sides.

❁ Carrot Cake

½ cup unsweetened coconut

6 ounces crushed pineapple with juice (one 8-ounce can)

½ cup butter or margarine

1 teaspoon **powdered stevia extract**

3 tablespoons date sugar

2 eggs, warmed to room temperature and beaten

⅓ cup plain nonfat yogurt

¼ cup soymilk or milk

1 teaspoon vanilla extract

½ teaspoon maple flavoring

½ cup chopped walnuts

2 cups grated carrots

1 cup whole wheat pastry flour

1 cup unbleached white flour

2 tablespoons soy flour

2 teaspoons baking powder

1 teaspoon baking soda

1½ teaspoons cinnamon

¼ teaspoon salt

- Preheat the oven to 350°F. Oil an 8 to 9-inch springform pan or a 6 x 10-inch cake pan.

- Soak the coconut in the pineapple and juice. Use all the juice from an 8-ounce can of pineapple but only 6 ounces of the pineapple. Set aside.

- Soften and cream the butter or margarine in a large mixing bowl. Cream in the stevia extract and the date sugar. Gradually cream in the beaten eggs. Don't worry if the butter separates.

- Thin the yogurt with the soymilk or milk and add to the butter mixture. Mix in the vanilla and maple flavoring. Stir in the walnuts, the coconut-pineapple mixture, and carrots.

- Sift the flours, leavenings, cinnamon, and salt together twice in a separate bowl.

- Fold the dry ingredients into the wet ingredients, stirring just until blended. The batter will be stiff.

- Spoon the batter into the cake pan, and bake for 1 hour. Cool in the pan.

- Release the pan and top with Cream Cheese Frosting (page 162).

Yield:
10 servings

Per serving:
(without frosting)
Calories 348
Total Fat 23 g
Sat. Fat 13 g
Protein 8 g
Carb. 31 g
Fiber 5 g
Sodium 300 mg

❀ Banana Cake

¼ cup oil

2 large eggs

⅓ cup plain nonfat yogurt

2 large ripe bananas, mashed

½ teaspoon **powdered stevia extract**

½ teaspoon vanilla

¾ cup whole wheat pastry flour

¾ cup unbleached white flour

½ teaspoon baking soda

1½ teaspoons baking powder

Pinch of salt

• Preheat the oven to 350°F. Oil and flour an 8-inch square or 9-inch round pan.

• Beat the oil and eggs together in a mixing bowl with a wire whisk or hand mixer. Mix in the yogurt, mashed bananas, stevia extract, and vanilla.

• Sift the flours, leavenings, and salt together. Gently fold the dry ingredients into the wet. Stir just until well mixed.

• Spoon the batter into the pan. Smooth the top with a spatula. Bake for 25 to 30 minutes.

SERVING SUGGESTION: *Serve topped with fresh, sliced, stevia-sweetened strawberries and a whipped topping or a warm Berry Sauce (page 156).*

Yield:
8 servings

Per serving:
Calories 195
Total Fat 9 g
Sat. Fat 1 g
Protein 5 g
Carb. 24 g
Fiber 3 g
Sodium 184 mg

Cookies and Bars

❋ *Helpful Hints* ❋

* Bring ingredients to room temperature. Preheat the oven well.

* Add just enough flour so that the dough pulls away from the sides of the bowl. If the batter seems too sticky, add 1 or 2 tablespoons more flour.

* When grinding nuts use a dry blender. In the following recipes grind the nuts first, then measure.

* Chilling the batter for several hours makes the dough easier to handle. The dough won't be sticky and less flour will be needed if rolling and cutting out the cookies. Plus the stevia will have more time to blend with the other ingredients.

* Even a half hour helps if you're short on time. Put the dough in the freezer for faster chilling or wrap well to bake later.

* Cookies rolled out thinner and cooked at a higher temperature (400°F) should be crispier. Several of these cookie recipes will be more cake-like.

* Adding a couple of tablespoons of date sugar will make the cookies crispier.

* Try to have a uniform size and thickness to your cookies.

* Keep a close watch on cookies. Since the cooking time is so short and ovens vary, cookies can easily overcook.

✿ REFRIGERATOR CUTTER COOKIES

½ cup butter or margarine, softened

2 large eggs, warmed to room temperature

¾ teaspoon **powdered stevia extract**

1 teaspoon vanilla extract

2 tablespoons maple syrup (optional)

Scant 1⅔ cups whole wheat pastry flour

½ cup ground raw nuts

1 teaspoon baking powder

⅛ teaspoon salt

• Soften and cream the butter or margarine in a mixing bowl.

• Cream the eggs into the butter. Mix in the stevia extract, vanilla, and maple syrup.

• Mix the flour, nut meal, baking powder, and salt together in a bowl. Stir the flour mixture into the butter mixture. Add flour until dough balls up and stops sticking to the sides of the bowl. Be careful not to add too much flour.

• Refrigerate the dough for at least 3 to 4 hours. Preheat the oven to 375°F. Oil a cookie sheet. Roll out the dough on a lightly floured board, and cut with cookie cutters. Bake for 12 minutes.

Yield:
20 (2½-inch)
cookies

Per serving:
Calories 110
Total Fat 8 g
Sat. Fat 3 g
Protein 3 g
Carb. 8 g
Fiber 2 g
Sodium 88 mg

VARIATIONS:
   (1) Add grated lemon peel and 1 teaspoon lemon juice.
   (2) Add grated orange peel and ½ teaspoon almond extract.

✻ MOLASSES COOKIES

¼ cup oil

2 tablespoons sesame tahini or
    cashew butter

1 tablespoon date sugar (optional)

¼ cup apple butter

¼ teaspoon **powdered stevia extract**

¾ teaspoon **stevia concentrate**

1½ tablespoons blackstrap molasses

1 teaspoon vanilla extract

1 cup whole wheat pastry flour

¼ teaspoon baking soda

¼ teaspoon salt

½ teaspoon cinnamon

¼ teaspoon ginger

⅛ teaspoon cloves

• Preheat the oven to 400°F. Oil a cookie sheet.

• Mix the oil and tahini or cashew butter together in a mixing bowl. Mix in the date sugar. Add the apple butter, stevia extract, stevia concentrate, molasses, and vanilla. Mix well.

• Mix the flour, leavening, salt, and spices together in a bowl. Mix the dry ingredients into the wet ingredients. Chill the batter for better handling.

• Roll out onto a floured cutting board. Flour the rolling pin. Use cookie cutters. Place the cookies on the baking sheet, and bake for 10 to 12 minutes. Thinner cookies will be crisper.

NOTE: *If you don't have the stevia concentrate use ½ teaspoon powdered stevia extract and 2 tablespoons molasses. If you don't want to use the molasses, use a total of 1 teaspoon of stevia concentrate, ¼ teaspoon powdered stevia extract and about 1 extra tablespoon of apple butter.*

Yield:
16 cookies

Per cookie:
Calories 85
Total Fat 5 g
Sat. Fat 0 g
Protein 2 g
Carb. 9 g
Fiber 1 g
Sodium 55 mg

✿ ALMOND DELIGHTS

½ cup finely ground raw almonds

3 ounces soft or regular tofu or
   1 large egg

⅓ cup orange juice

⅓ cup almond butter

⅓ cup oil

2 tablespoons date sugar (optional)

1 teaspoon almond extract

½ teaspoon **powdered stevia extract**

Grated rind of 1 orange

1 cup whole wheat pastry flour

¼ teaspoon baking soda

½ teaspoon baking powder

¼ teaspoon salt

• Preheat the oven to 375°F. Oil a cookie sheet.

• Grind the almonds to a fine meal in the blender. Place in a bowl and set aside.

• Blend the tofu and orange juice in the blender.

• Cream the almond butter and oil together in a mixing bowl. Stir in the date sugar, almond extract, stevia extract, and grated orange rind. Add the blended tofu (or egg) and mix well.

• Stir the almond meal, flour, leavenings, and salt together in a bowl. Add the flour mixture to the wet ingredients. Add just enough flour so that the batter stops sticking to the sides of the bowl and forms a ball. Chill the dough for easier handling.

• Roll the dough into small balls with your hands and, place on the cookie sheet. Flatten the cookies to about ¼-inch thick with the palm of your hand. Press ½ almond, cut lengthwise, in the center of each cookie. Bake for 12 to 15 minutes.

Yield:
16 cookies

Per cookie:
Calories 135
Total Fat 9 g
Sat. Fat 1 g
Protein 5 g
Carb. 9 g
Fiber 1 g
Sodium 94 mg

❁ CHOCOLATE CHIP COOKIES

½ cup butter or margarine, softened

½ cup cashew butter or almond butter

2 tablespoons date sugar (optional)

¼ cup unsweetened applesauce or mashed banana

1 large egg

⅓ teaspoon **powdered stevia extract**

½ teaspoon **stevia concentrate**

1 teaspoon vanilla extract

1 cup whole wheat pastry flour

½ teaspoon baking soda

¼ teaspoon salt

½ cup chocolate chips or carob chips

• Preheat the oven to 375°F. Oil a cookie sheet.

• Soften the butter or margarine. Cream the butter and cashew butter or almond butter together. Mix in the date sugar. Blend in the applesauce or mashed banana. Beat in the egg. Mix in the stevia extract, stevia concentrate, and vanilla.

Yield:
about 18
(2½-inch)
cookies

Per cookie:
Calories 146
Total Fat 11 g
Sat. Fat 5 g
Protein 3 g
Carb. 10 g
Fiber 1 g
Sodium 124 mg

• Stir the flour, baking soda, and salt together, and mix into the liquid ingredients. Add the chocolate or carob chips, and stir. The batter should be fairly stiff. Add a little more flour if necessary (1 or 2 tablespoons). You can chill the dough for easier handling.

• Drop the dough by the spoonful onto the cookie sheet. Press down on the cookies once with your palm. Bake for 12 to 15 minutes.

FOR A REDUCED FAT, VEGAN COOKIE, USE:

½ cup cashew butter

¼ cup oil

½ cup apple butter

⅓ teaspoon **stevia extract**

½ teaspoon **stevia concentrate**

1 teaspoon vanilla

1 cup whole wheat flour

¼ teaspoon baking soda

¼ teaspoon salt

⅓ cup chips

Yield:
16 cookies

Per cookie:
Calories 145
Total Fat 9 g
Sat. Fat 2 g
Protein 3 g
Carb. 14 g
Fiber 1 g
Sodium 54 mg

✳ Jam Dot Cookies

⅓ cup oil

1 egg

2 tablespoons apple butter

3 tablespoons plain nonfat yogurt

2 tablespoons date sugar (optional)

1 teaspoon vanilla

½ teaspoon **powdered stevia extract**

1½ cups whole wheat pastry flour

¼ teaspoon baking soda

⅛ teaspoon salt

About ½ cup jam or other filling

• In a mixing bowl, whip the oil and egg together. Mix in the apple butter, yogurt, date sugar, vanilla, and stevia extract.

• Stir the flour, baking soda, and salt together. Mix the dry ingredients into the wet ingredients. The batter should start to pull away from the sides of the bowl.

• Refrigerate the dough for at least 2 hours.

• Preheat the oven to 325°F. Butter a cookie sheet. Remove the batter from the refrigerator. Form into 1-inch balls and place on the cookie sheet. Flatten the balls slightly with your palm. Make a depression in the center of the cookies. (The tip of a honey dipper works great. Dip it in flour to keep it from sticking.) Spoon some jam or other filling into the depression. Bake for 15 to 20 minutes.

Yield:
about 20
cookies

Per cookie:
Calories 95
Total Fat 4 g
Sat. Fat 0 g
Protein 2 g
Carb. 13 g
Fiber 1 g
Sodium 37 mg

✻ CASHEW COCONUT CHEWS

⅔ cup unsweetened coconut

6 ounces pineapple juice

1 tablespoon sesame tahini

2 tablespoons maple syrup (optional)

1 teaspoon vanilla extract

½ teaspoon **powdered stevia extract**

½ cup coarsely ground raw cashews

Scant ⅔ cup whole wheat pastry flour

• Preheat the oven to 350°F. Oil a cookie sheet.

• Soak the coconut in the pineapple juice in a small bowl.

• Cream together the tahini, maple syrup, vanilla, and stevia extract in a mixing bowl. Stir in the soaked coconut and ground cashews. Mix in the flour.

• Drop the batter by the spoonful onto an oiled cookie sheet using two spoons. Leave the cookies dome-shaped. Bake for about 25 minutes.

Yield:
16 (1½-inch)
cookies

Per cookie:
Calories 117
Total Fat 9 g
Sat. Fat 6 g
Protein 2 g
Carb. 7 g
Fiber 2 g
Sodium 5 mg

✻ Coconut Fig Chews

½ cup chopped figs

½ cup unsweetened fruit juice or water

1 cup unsweetened coconut

½ cup ground sesame seeds

⅛ teaspoon salt

½ teaspoon **powdered stevia extract**

2 tablespoons cashew butter

⅓ cup whole wheat pastry flour

- Preheat the oven to 350°F. Oil a cookie sheet.
- Stew the chopped figs in the fruit juice or water for 8 to 10 minutes. Add the coconut to the pan, mix, and set aside.
- Grind the sesame seeds in a blender. In a mixing bowl, place the stewed figs and coconut, ground sesame seeds, salt, stevia extract, cashew butter, and flour. Mix well. Shape the cookies with your hands. Place on the cookie sheet and flatten slightly.
- Bake for 12 to 14 minutes.

NOTE: *You may add 1 teaspoon of powdered stevia herb.*

Yield:
16 (1½-inch)
cookies

Per cookie:
Calories 200
Total Fat 15 g
Sat. Fat 11 g
Protein 3 g
Carb. 15 g
Fiber 5 g
Sodium 32 mg

✳ DATE NUT COOKIES

2 large chopped dates

⅓ cup apple juice or water

1 cup ground walnuts

¼ cup oil

½ teaspoon **powdered stevia extract**

1 teaspoon vanilla extract

¼ cup apple butter

¾ cup whole wheat pastry flour

1 teaspoon cinnamon

• Preheat the oven to 350°F. Oil a cookie sheet.

• Simmer the chopped dates in the juice or water for 10 to 15 minutes in a small pan.

• Grind the walnuts in the blender to a coarse meal. Put in a bowl and set aside.

• Coarsely grind the softened dates and the liquid in the blender.

• Beat the oil, stevia extract, vanilla, and apple butter together in a mixing bowl. Add the liquefied dates and mix. Stir in the ground walnuts, flour, and cinnamon.

• Drop the batter by the spoonful onto a cookie sheet using two spoons. Make small dome-shaped cookies. Bake for 15 to 20 minutes.

NOTE: *You may use any combination of nuts and seeds instead of walnuts.*

Yield:
12 cookies

Per cookie:
Calories 116
Total Fat 8 g
Sat. Fat 1 g
Protein 2 g
Carb. 9 g
Fiber 1 g
Sodium 1 mg

✳ CRISSCROSS
PEANUT BUTTER COOKIES

¼ cup butter or margarine, softened

⅔ cup natural peanut butter

½ teaspoon **powdered stevia extract**

2 tablespoons date sugar (optional)

½ teaspoon maple flavoring

¼ cup apple butter

1 large egg

¾ cup whole wheat pastry flour

½ teaspoon baking soda

½ teaspoon cinnamon

⅛ teaspoon salt

- Preheat the oven to 350°F. Oil a cookie sheet.
- Soften and cream the butter or margarine in a mixing bowl. Cream the peanut butter into the butter. Mix in the stevia extract, date sugar, maple flavoring, and apple butter. Beat in the egg until thick and smooth.
- Stir the flour, baking soda, cinnamon, and salt together in a bowl. Add the flour mixture to the peanut butter mixture.

Yield:
16 large
cookies

Per cookie:
Calories 123
Total Fat 8 g
Sat. Fat 3 g
Protein 4 g
Carb. 8 g
Fiber 2 g
Sodium 114 mg

• Place large balls of batter on the cookie sheet using two spoons. Flatten each cookie with a floured fork, making a crisscross pattern.

• Bake for 12 minutes.

FOR VEGAN PEANUT BUTTER COOKIES, USE:

¼ cup oil

⅔ cup peanut butter

⅓ cup apple butter

2 ounces tofu (mix the tofu with the apple butter in a blender first)

½ teaspoon **stevia extract**

2 tablespoons date sugar (optional)

½ teaspoon maple flavoring

¾ cup whole wheat pastry flour

½ teaspoon baking soda

½ teaspoon cinnamon

⅛ teaspoon salt

Yield:
16 large cookies

Per cookie:
Calories 123
Total Fat 8 g
Sat. Fat 1 g
Protein 4 g
Carb. 8 g
Fiber 2 g
Sodium 79 mg

✳ Oatmeal Raisin Cookies

½ cup loosely packed raisins

½ cup apple juice

⅓ cup oil

2 tablespoons sesame tahini or
  almond butter

1 large egg

2 tablespoons plain nonfat yogurt

2 tablespoons date sugar (optional)

⅓ teaspoon **powdered stevia
  extract**

½ teaspoon **stevia concentrate**

1 teaspoon vanilla extract

1 cup rolled oats

1 cup whole wheat pastry flour

¼ teaspoon baking soda

½ teaspoon baking powder

1 teaspoon cinnamon

¼ teaspoon salt

¼ cup chopped walnuts (optional)

- Preheat the oven to 375°F. Oil a cookie sheet.

- Place the raisins and apple juice in a small pan, and simmer over low heat for 10 to 15 minutes. Set aside.

- In a mixing bowl, beat the oil and tahini or almond butter together. Mix in the egg then the yogurt. Stir in the date sugar, stevia extract, stevia concentrate, and vanilla.

- Grind the oats in a blender. (Only pulse 2 to 3 times and do ⅓ cup at a time.) Remove from blender. Cream half of the stewed raisins and all of the juice in a blender. Set the rest of the raisins aside. Stir the creamed raisins into the other ingredients.

- Mix the ground oats, flour, leavenings, cinnamon, and salt. together. Mix into the wet ingredients. Add the rest of the raisins and the walnuts, if desired. Don't over-mix.

- Drop onto the oiled cookie sheet, and flatten with the palm of your hand. Bake for 13 to 15 minutes.

Yield:
16 (3-inch)
cookies

Per cookie:
Calories 121
Total Fat 6 g
Sat. Fat 1 g
Protein 3 g
Carb. 14 g
Fiber 2 g
Sodium 73 mg

# SESAME CRISPS

3 to 4 tablespoons oil

¾ cup cashew or almond butter

½ cup apple butter

2 tablespoons maple syrup (optional)

½ teaspoon **powdered stevia extract**

½ teaspoon maple flavoring

1 teaspoon vanilla extract

1½ cups raw sesame seeds

⅓ cup whole wheat flour

¼ teaspoon salt

• Preheat the oven to 375°F. Oil a large baking pan (about 9 x 13-inch) or a small cookie sheet with sides.

• In a small bowl, blend the oil into the nut butter. (If the nut butter is very thick, use the larger amount of oil. If it is thin, use the lesser amount.) Mix in the apple butter, maple syrup, stevia extract, maple flavoring, and vanilla.

• Place the sesame seeds in a large mixing bowl. Stir in the nut butter mixture. Add the flour and salt, and mix well.

• Press the mixture evenly and firmly into the bottom of the pan or cookie sheet to about ¼ inch thick. Bake for 15 to 18 minutes.

• Cool completely before cutting.

Yield:
30 servings

Per serving:
Calories 109
Total Fat 8 g
Sat. Fat 1 g
Protein 3 g
Carb. 7 g
Fiber 1 g
Sodium 20 mg

TROPICAL FRUIT BARS

CRUST

½ cup finely ground raw cashews
½ cup whole wheat flour
Pinch of salt
¼ teaspoon **powdered stevia extract**
3 tablespoons oil

• Preheat the oven to 350°F. Oil an 8-inch square or 6 x 10-inch pan.

• Grind the cashews in a blender. Mix the cashews, flour, salt, and stevia extract together in a bowl. Stir the oil in with a fork until it is evenly distributed. Press the mixture firmly into the pan. Bake for 12 to 15 minutes. Cool.

MIDDLE LAYER

4 large dates, chopped
¼ cup water

• Simmer the dates in the water until they become a creamy paste (about 5 to 10 minutes). Add a little more water if it is too thick. Spread the date paste in a thin layer over the cooled crust.

• Reduce the oven temperature to 325°F.

FILLING

1 (8-ounce) can crushed pineapple

1 medium ripe banana

1 teaspoon vanilla extract

½ teaspoon **powdered stevia extract**

¼ cup flour

½ cup unsweetened coconut

• In a blender cream the pineapple (with juice), banana, vanilla, and stevia extract together. Pour into a mixing bowl. Gently stir in the flour and coconut. Pour the filling evenly over the crust. Bake for 45 to 50 minutes until a knife inserted near the edge comes out clean. Cool completely before cutting.

Yield:
16 bars

Per bar:
Calories 139
Total Fat 10 g
Sat. Fat 5 g
Protein 2 g
Carb. 13 g
Fiber 2 g
Sodium 4 mg

✱ PEANUT BUTTER BARS

These are sure to please.

½ cup natural peanut butter

⅓ cup oil

¼ cup apple butter

2 tablespoons date sugar (optional)

½ teaspoon **powdered stevia extract**

1 teaspoon vanilla

2 tablespoons soft tofu or 1 egg

1 cup whole wheat pastry flour

½ cup rolled oats (quick-cooking are O.K.)

½ teaspoon baking soda

¼ teaspoon salt

• Preheat the oven to 350°F. Oil an 11 x 7-inch or similar size baking pan.

• Mix the peanut butter and oil together in a bowl. If your peanut butter is already runny, reduce the oil and increase the peanut butter some. Mix in the apple butter, date sugar, stevia extract, vanilla, and tofu or egg. The tofu may be blended first in a blender or creamed directly into the batter until smooth.

• Stir in the flour, oats, baking soda, and salt. Press the batter into the bottom of the pan, and bake for 25 minutes.

✳ CAROB PEANUT BUTTER FROSTING

½ cup carob powder
¾ cup soymilk or milk
⅓ teaspoon **powdered stevia extract**
⅓ cup peanut butter
1 teaspoon vanilla

• Mix the carob, soymilk or milk, and stevia extract together in a saucepan. Cook at a low boil for about 7 minutes. Remove from the heat and mix in the peanut butter and vanilla until smooth.

• Remove the bars from the oven, and frost immediately. Cool before cutting.

NOTE: *You may use half carob and half cocoa (or 1 square of baker's chocolate, melted) plus 2 tablespoons honey.*

Yield:
25 servings

Per serving:
Calories 118
Total Fat 7 g
Sat. Fat 1 g
Protein 4 g
Carb. 10 g
Fiber 2 g
Sodium 70 mg

 DATE BARS

CRUST AND TOPPING

¾ cup rolled oats

1 cup whole wheat pastry flour

¼ cup unsweetened coconut

¼ teaspoon **powdered stevia extract**

⅛ teaspoon salt

6 tablespoons oil

½ teaspoon maple flavoring or
2 tablespoons maple syrup

• Preheat the oven to 350°F. Oil an 8-inch square or 6 x 10-inch pan.

• Mix the oats, flour, coconut, stevia extract, and salt in a mixing bowl. Stir the oil and maple flavoring into the dry ingredients. If using the maple syrup rub in with your fingers.

• Press about ⅔ of the mixture firmly into the bottom of the baking pan. Save the rest for the topping.

FILLING

1½ cups chopped dates
(not packed)

About ⅔ cup water

Pinch of salt

⅓ teaspoon **powdered
stevia extract**

• Place all the ingredients in a small saucepan, and cook over low heat until creamy. Add a little more water if necessary. (It should be a thick, creamy, spreadable paste.)

• Spread the date filling over the crust. Sprinkle the topping over the filling. Press the topping lightly into the filling with a fork.

• Bake for 30 minutes. Cool thoroughly before cutting.

Yield:
16 bars

Per bar:
Calories 167
Total Fat 8 g
Sat. Fat 3 g
Protein 2 g
Carb. 23 g
Fiber 3 g
Sodium 18 mg

✵ Pumpkin Bars

1 large egg

2 tablespoons soymilk or milk

⅓ cup oil

¼ cup apple butter

⅓ teaspoon **powdered stevia extract**

½ teaspoon **stevia concentrate**
  or 1 tablespoon molasses

¼ teaspoon maple flavoring

1 tablespoon date sugar (optional)

1 packed cup cooked pumpkin or
  squash

1½ cups whole wheat pastry flour

1½ teaspoons baking powder

1 teaspoon cinnamon

¼ teaspoon cloves

¼ teaspoon nutmeg

¼ teaspoon salt

¼ cup chopped sunflower seeds
  (optional)

• Preheat the oven to 350°F. Oil an 8-inch shallow square pan.

• Lightly beat the egg and soymilk or milk in a small bowl. Beat the oil in a large mixing bowl with the apple butter, stevia extract, stevia concentrate or molasses, maple flavoring, and date sugar. Stir in the beaten egg. Gently mix in the pumpkin or squash.

• Sift the flour, baking powder, spices, and salt together. Fold the dry ingredients into the wet. Add the sunflower seeds just before the flour is completely blended. The batter will be fairly stiff.

• Spoon the batter into the pan, Bake for 30 to 35 minutes.

SERVING SUGGESTION: *Top with Lemon Icing (page 161) or Cream Cheese Frosting (page 162).*

Yield:
16 bars

Per bar:
Calories 104
Total Fat 5 g
Sat. Fat 0 g
Protein 2 g
Carb. 12 g
Fiber 2 g
Sodium 13 mg

✻ GRANOLA ENERGY BARS

2 teaspoons powdered stevia leaf

2 cups granola (Use your favorite; if it has chopped nuts and dried fruit, all the better.)

⅓ cup tahini, cashew, or almond butter

2 tablespoons oil

⅓ cup apple butter

1 tablespoon honey (optional)

⅓ teaspoon **powdered stevia extract**

1 teaspoon vanilla

• Preheat the oven to 375°F. Oil a 6 x 10-inch baking dish.

• Mix the powdered stevia leaf into the granola in a large mixing bowl.

• In a small bowl, mix the nut butter and oil together. Add the apple butter, honey, stevia extract, and vanilla. Gently stir this mixture into the granola.

• Press the batter firmly and evenly into the baking dish. Bake for 18 to 20 minutes. Cool completely before cutting.

OPTION: *Add 1 or 2 heaping tablespoons protein powder to the batter.*

Yield:
20 servings

Per serving:
Calories 95
Total Fat 5 g
Sat. Fat 1 g
Protein 2 g
Carb. 10 g
Fiber 1 g
Sodium 29 mg

✤ Pecan Sandies

6 tablespoons butter or margarine, softened

2 tablespoons sesame tahini

2 tablespoons date sugar (optional)

½ teaspoon **powdered stevia extract**

1 teaspoon vanilla extract

2 tablespoons soymilk or milk

2 large eggs, lightly beaten

1¼ cups whole wheat pastry flour

¼ teaspoon salt

½ teaspoon baking powder

½ cup coarsely ground pecans

⅓ cup chopped pecans

15 pecan halves

• Cream the softened butter or margarine with the tahini, date sugar, stevia extract, and vanilla in a mixing bowl. Lightly beat the soymilk or milk with the eggs, and mix into the batter.

• Sift the flour, salt, and baking powder together. Coarsely grind the pecans in a blender, and measure out ½ cup. Chop the pecans and measure out ⅓ cup. Mix the flour, ground pecans, and chopped pecans into the batter. The batter should pull away from the sides of the bowl. If the batter is too sticky, add 1 or 2 tablespoons more flour. Be careful not to add too much flour.

• Refrigerate the batter for several hours or more.

• Preheat the oven to 350°F. Oil a cookie sheet.

• Shape the dough into balls with your hands. Flatten the balls with the palm of your hand on the cookie sheet. Press a pecan half in the center of each cookie. Bake for 15 minutes.

Yield:
18 cookies

Per cookie:
Calories 120
Total Fat 9 g
Sat. Fat 3 g
Protein 3 g
Carb. 8 g
Fiber 2 g
Sodium 90 mg

✳ Carob Brownies

½ cup oil

4 ounces soft or firm tofu

¾ cup unsweetened applesauce

½ teaspoon **powdered stevia extract**

1 teaspoon vanilla extract

1 tablespoon lemon juice

½ cup carob powder*

Scant 1¼ cups whole wheat pastry flour

½ teaspoon baking soda

1 teaspoon baking powder

¼ teaspoon salt

½ cup chopped walnuts (optional)

Yield:
16 brownies

Per brownie:
Calories 124
Total Fat 8 g
Sat. Fat 1 g
Protein 2 g
Carb. 12 g
Fiber 2 g
Sodium 96 mg

• Preheat the oven to 350°F. Oil an 8-inch, shallow square pan.

• Place the oil, tofu, applesauce, stevia extract, vanilla, and lemon juice into a blender. Blend until smooth and pour into a large mixing bowl. Stir in the carob powder until well blended (a hand mixer will help). When measuring the carob, tamp the cup on the counter a few times.

• Sift the flour, leavenings, and salt together. Fold the dry ingredients into the wet. Mix in the walnuts. Don't over-mix. Spoon the batter into the pan, and smooth the top. Bake for 25 to 30 minutes.

TO BAKE WITH EGG, USE:

½ cup oil

1 egg

¼ cup plain nonfat yogurt

½ cup applesauce

¼ cup apple butter

½ teaspoon **powdered stevia extract**

1 teaspoon vanilla

1 teaspoon lemon juice

½ cup carob powder

1¼ cups whole wheat flour

½ teaspoon baking soda

1 teaspoon baking powder

¼ teaspoon salt

Yield:
16 brownies

Per brownie:
Calories 130
Total Fat 8 g
Sat. Fat 6 g
Protein 2 g
Carb. 13 g
Fiber 2 g
Sodium 37 mg

OPTION: *Replace ½ cup carob powder with ¼ cup carob powder and ¼ cup cocoa plus 2 tablespoons honey.*

*Read about carob types on page 180 in Food Preparation Tips.

✻ CHOCOLATE BROWNIES

4 squares unsweetened baker's
  chocolate

6 tablespoons butter or margarine,
  softened

½ cup low-fat cottage cheese

¼ cup honey or maple syrup

2 tablespoons date sugar

¼ cup apple butter

¾ teaspoon **powdered stevia extract**

1 teaspoon vanilla extract

2 large eggs

1 cup whole wheat pastry flour

½ teaspoon baking soda

¼ teaspoon salt

½ cup chopped walnuts

• Preheat the oven to 350°F. Oil an 8-inch, shallow square pan.

• Melt the chocolate over low heat in a heavy-bottomed pan
or double boiler.

• Soften and cream the butter or margarine in a mixing bowl.
Stir in the melted chocolate.

• Put the cottage cheese through a fine-mesh strainer, then
mix into the butter and chocolate. Blend in the honey or
maple syrup and the date sugar. Mix in the apple butter, stevia extract, and vanilla. Beat the eggs in one at a time.

• Mix the flour, baking soda, and salt together. Stir the dry
ingredients into the wet until blended. Mix in the walnuts.

• Spoon the batter into the pan, and bake for 35 to 40 minutes.

Yield:
16 servings

Per brownie:
Calories 177
Total Fat 12 g
Sat. Fat 6 g
Protein 4 g
Carb. 17 g
Fiber 2 g
Sodium 157 mg

Custards, Crepes, Puddings, Pies

❧ *Helpful Hints* ❧

* Egg custards can be difficult to make. It all depends on not overcooking and not cooking at too high of a temperature. Below are some suggestions.

  –Know your oven. If it runs hot keep the temperature at the lower setting of 300°F.

  –Check the water bath through the oven window to make sure it doesn't boil.

  –Place the rack below the center of the oven to keep the top from forming a crust or browning.

  –Remove the custard from the oven when a knife inserted halfway down at the side of the pan comes out clean. The custard will continue cooking as it cools on the counter.

* In tofu puddings either soft or firm tofu can be used, but a pie filling will set better if firm is used.

* Use only fresh tofu. Tofu in aseptic cartons tastes fresh and is great to use in dessert recipes.

* When using cornstarch to thicken puddings, make sure the starch is cooked. Slowly bring the pudding to a boil. After it starts boiling, reduce the heat to low and simmer 5 to 7 minutes longer, stirring occasionally. Don't add starch to hot liquid directly. Mix it into some of the cold liquid first before adding it to the hot liquid.

* Quick tapioca pellets have to sit in the cold ingredients before cooking. Let it sit 5 minutes for milk and 15 minutes for acid fruits, then bring it to a full boil. Make sure the white pellets have turned clear before taking it off the heat; simmer until they do. Tapioca thickens as it cools.

* In making pie crusts, all the ingredients must be cold. It may help to roll out the dough if it is chilled first. Chill in the refrigerator for 20 minutes and then bring it out on the counter for 5 minutes before rolling out. The crust can also be chilled for 20 minutes after it is rolled out and put into the pan. This helps keep the crust from shrinking as much during baking.

* Crusts with fillings, like pumpkin pie, can be partially baked before adding the filling to prevent creating a soggy crust. Bake for 15 minutes at 350°F. Take the crust out of the oven, cool, fill, and return to the oven.

* There are other techniques to making good crusts and pies. I recommend the book *Fruit Sweet and Sugar Free* for detailed instructions. The author, Janice Feuer, is a professional baker and pastry chef.

 # FLAN

4 fresh, large eggs

2 cups soymilk or milk

1 teaspoon vanilla extract

¾ teaspoon **powdered stevia extract**

1 tablespoon flour

Pinch of salt

3 tablespoons rice syrup
   or barley malt

• Preheat the oven to 325°F. Have ready an 8-inch, shallow, straight-sided, glass or ceramic baking dish and a larger pan for a water bath. Place an oven rack below the center of the oven.

• Place the eggs, milk, vanilla, stevia extract, flour, and salt in a blender. Process on low for several minutes. Set aside.

• Heat the rice syrup or barley malt in a small saucepan to a rolling boil. Spoon into the bottom of the baking dish, and quickly roll around to coat the bottom and sides. (You may have to use a spatula to help spread it around.) Caramelize sugar if that is all that is available, or omit.

• After the caramel glaze has cooled and hardened, pour in the custard. If it is frothy, pour the mixture through a strainer while pouring into the baking dish and/or spoon off the froth. Place the baking dish in a water bath by filling a larger pan with 1 inch of warm water. The water in the bath must not boil. If 325° is too hot, reduce the oven temperature.

• Bake approximately 1 hour. Check to see if it is done by inserting a knife halfway in near the sides of the dish. If the knife comes out clean, remove the custard from the oven.

• Cool on a rack for 1 hour, then turn out onto a plate. Loosen the sides of the custard first, if necessary. Refrigerate several hours before serving.

Yield:
8 servings

Per serving:
Calories 93
Total Fat 4 g
Sat. Fat 2 g
Protein 6 g
Carb. 9 g
Fiber 0 g
Sodium 94 mg

Banana Coconut Custard

Light and delicate in flavor and texture

1½ cups soymilk or milk
1 large ripe banana
2 large eggs
¼ cup unsweetened coconut
1 teaspoon vanilla extract
½ teaspoon **powdered stevia extract**
Pinch of salt
Sprinkle of nutmeg

• Preheat the oven to 325°F. Have ready 4 individual custard cups (glass or ceramic, ½-cup size) and a baking dish filled 1 inch deep with warm water.

• Blend all the ingredients, except the nutmeg, together in a blender on low. If frothy, pour the mixture through a strainer while pouring into the dishes, or spoon off the froth. Sprinkle the tops with nutmeg.

• Place the custard cups in the water bath. Bake for 45 to 50 minutes until a knife inserted near the side of the dish comes out clean. Remove from the oven and chill on a rack. Serve immediately or refrigerate.

Yield:
4 servings

Per serving:
Calories 203
Total Fat 14 g
Sat. Fat 10 g
Protein 7 g
Carb. 15 g
Fiber 3 g
Sodium 149 mg

 # CREPES

Simple but elegant

2 large eggs
1 cup soymilk or milk
Scant ¾ cup whole wheat pastry flour
2 teaspoons oil
Dash of salt
Pinch of **powdered stevia extract**

• Blend all the ingredients together in a blender on low. If the mixture is frothy, let it sit covered in the blender for 5 to 10 minutes.

• Pour approximately ¼ cup of the batter at a time into a 6-inch, heated, lightly oiled, heavy-bottomed frying pan. A non-stick pan works well. Tilt the pan until the batter reaches all sides. When the bottom is lightly browned, flip the crepe and lightly brown the other side. Crepes are best when thin.

• Serve filled with Apple or Pear Filling (page 158) or Plum Sauce (page 153) and rolled up.

Yield:
8 crepes

Per crepe:
Calories 84
Total Fat 3 g
Sat. Fat 1 g
Protein 4 g
Carb. 9 g
Fiber 2 g
Sodium 51 mg

BANANA DATE PUDDING

4 large dates

1 pound silken tofu, soft or firm

4 tablespoons oil

½ teaspoon **powdered stevia extract**

1½ teaspoons vanilla extract

2 ripe medium to large bananas, chopped

• Chop the dates and place them in a blender or food processor. Add part of the tofu and oil, and grind the mixture. Add more tofu and oil along with the stevia extract, vanilla, and bananas. Blend until creamy. Use the pulse button, stirring between pulses. If using a food processor, place all the ingredients in the container at once, and process until smooth.

• Spoon into dessert glasses or bowls. Chill 1 to 2 hours.

Yield:
4 servings

Per serving:
Calories 206
Total Fat 10 g
Sat. Fat 1 g
Protein 8 g
Carb. 23 g
Fiber 3 g
Sodium 39 mg

Vanilla Pudding

2 tablespoons arrowroot powder or cornstarch

2 tablespoons whole wheat pastry flour

½ teaspoon **powdered stevia extract**

Pinch of salt

2 cups vanilla-flavored soymilk

• Mix the arrowroot powder or cornstarch, flour, stevia extract, and salt together in a cup or small bowl. Make a paste with some of the soymilk. Gradually thin out the paste until it will pour. Remove any lumps.

• Gently heat the rest of the milk on low heat. Slowly add the thickeners, stirring gently with a wooden spatula or spoon. Simmer over low heat for 3 to 5 minutes. The mixture will thicken quickly if using arrowroot powder. If using cornstarch, cook the pudding on low long enough to make sure the starch is cooked (about 7 to 10 minutes).

• Spoon the pudding into dessert glasses or bowls.

NOTE: *If using plain soymilk or dairy milk, add 2 teaspoons vanilla extract.*

Yield:
4 servings

Per serving:
Calories 69
Total Fat 2 g
Sat. Fat 0 g
Protein 4 g
Carb. 9 g
Fiber 2 g
Sodium 41 mg

❧ CHOCOLATE PUDDING

A smooth and sumptuous chocolate treat

1½ squares baker's chocolate

3 tablespoons honey or maple syrup

¾ teaspoon **powdered stevia extract**

3 cups soymilk or milk

Pinch of salt

2 to 3 tablespoons cornstarch

2 to 3 tablespoons flour

1 tablespoon vanilla extract

• Melt the chocolate squares on low heat in a heavy-bottomed pan or double boiler. Stir in the honey or maple syrup and the stevia extract. Gradually mix 2 cups of the soymilk or milk into the chocolate. Add a pinch of salt. Heat the mixture to just below the boiling point.

• While heating the milk, dissolve the cornstarch and flour in the remaining cup of milk. Smooth out any lumps. Gradually add the starches to the hot milk.

• Cook on medium low about 5 minutes until thick, stirring gently. Continue cooking on low 3 to 5 minutes longer. Remove from the heat and stir in the vanilla.

• If making a pie, cool the pudding first, then pour into a pre-baked 9-inch pie shell.

NOTE: *If preparing the recipe as a pie filling, use the larger amounts of cornstarch and flour so it will set better.*

Yield:
6 servings

Per serving:
Calories 132
Total Fat 6 g
Sat. Fat 0 g
Protein 5 g
Carb. 18 g
Fiber 1 g
Sodium 33 mg

 # CAROB PUDDING

Rich and silky smooth

½ cup carob powder
½ cup water
1 (12.3-ounce) box silken tofu, soft or firm
1 tablespoon oil
⅓ to ½ teaspoon **powdered stevia extract** (to taste)
1 large banana
½ teaspoon vanilla extract
Pinch of salt

• Place the carob powder and water in a small, heavy-bottomed pan. Cook at a low boil for 6 to 8 minutes, stirring constantly until thick and smooth. If too thick. add a little more water.

• Place the carob syrup and all the other ingredients in a blender or food processor, and blend until creamy. Spoon into dessert dishes and chill in the refrigerator about 1 hour or more.

Read about carob types on page 180 in Food Preparation Tips.

Yield:
4 servings

Per serving:
Calories 177
Total Fat 8 g
Sat. Fat 1 g
Protein 8 g
Carb. 21 g
Fiber 4 g
Sodium 34 mg

❧ SWEET POTATO RICE PUDDING

½ packed cup cooked sweet potatoes or yams

1⅔ cups soymilk or milk

½ teaspoon **powdered stevia extract**

2 cups cooked short–grain brown rice

1 teaspoon vanilla extract

¼ teaspoon cinnamon

Dash of cardamom (optional)

Pinch of salt

Yield:
4 servings

Per serving:
Calories 162
Total Fat 3 g
Sat. Fat 0 g
Protein 6 g
Carb. 29 g
Fiber 2 g
Sodium 44 mg

• To cook the sweet potatoes or yams: peel, cut into pieces, and steam. Blend the cooked sweet potato and soymilk or milk in a blender with the stevia extract.

• Place the rice in a medium-size, heavy-bottomed saucepan. Pour the blended potatoes and milk into the pan. Cook over medium-low heat for about 20 to 30 minutes or until the pudding is thick and creamy. Add the vanilla, spices, and salt, and stir. Cook a few minutes longer. Add a little more milk, and cook longer if necessary. This pudding is excellent served warm with Cashew Cream (page 165).

TO MAKE WITHOUT SWEET POTATOES, USE:

2 cups soymilk or milk

1 teaspoon lemon juice

½ teaspoon **stevia extract**

2 cups rice

¼ teaspoon cinnamon

Pinch of salt

CREAMY BAKED RICE PUDDING

Great to make on a cold day

1 teaspoon butter or margarine
½ cup uncooked, short-grain brown or white rice
3 cups soymilk or milk
½ teaspoon **powdered stevia extract**
1 tablespoon honey (optional)
1 tablespoon lemon juice
Finely grated rind of ½ lemon
¼ teaspoon cinnamon
¼ cup raisins (optional)

Yield:
6 servings

Per serving:
Calories 142
Total Fat 3 g
Sat. Fat 0 g
Protein 6 g
Carb. 23 g
Fiber .3 g
Sodium 22 mg

• Preheat the oven to 300°F. Butter a medium-size casserole dish with the butter or margarine.

• Place the uncooked rice in the casserole dish with half of the milk. Cover the dish and place it in the oven. Uncover after it starts boiling or in about 30 minutes.

• After about 1 hour, stir in the rest of the milk, the stevia extract, lemon juice, lemon rind, cinnamon, and raisins, if desired. Leave uncovered.

• Stir the rice about every half hour. Bake about 2 hours total until thick and creamy. Remove from the oven before all the milk is totally absorbed.

🌿 TAPIOCA PUDDING

2 cups soymilk or milk

3 tablespoons quick tapioca

⅓ to ½ teaspoon **powdered stevia extract**

½ teaspoon guar gum

1 tablespoon honey (optional)

1 teaspoon vanilla extract

4 ounces of soft tofu (optional)

• Use soymilk, whole milk, or 2% milk. Whisk the milk, tapioca, stevia extract, and guar gum together in a heavy-bottomed saucepan. Let the mixture sit for 5 minutes. Cook over medium-low heat. When hot, add the honey and stir continuously. Remove from the heat after a full boil is reached. Stir in the vanilla.

• Cool the mixture on the counter. To keep a skin from forming, cover the bowl with plastic wrap or waxed paper. If desired, blend the tofu until creamy and fold in. This is especially helpful if you don't have the guar gum. You can also use an egg instead of guar gum or tofu. Follow the directions on the back of the tapioca box, but eliminate the sugar.

• Spoon into individual serving bowls, and refrigerate until firm.

Yield:
4 servings

Per serving:
Calories 140
Total Fat 2 g
Sat. Fat 0 g
Protein 4 g
Carb. 28 g
Fiber 0 g
Sodium 124 mg

TAPIOCA BERRY PUDDING

2 cups fresh or frozen berries (sliced if using strawberries)

1½ cups apple juice

⅓ to ½ teaspoon **powdered stevia extract**

2 teaspoons lemon juice

3 tablespoons quick tapioca

1 tablespoon honey (optional)

6 to 8 ounces soft tofu

• Blend the berries, apple juice, stevia extract, and lemon juice together in a blender. Pass through a fine-mesh strainer to remove seeds.

• Pour into a heavy-bottomed saucepan. Whisk in the tapioca and let sit for 15 minutes. Cook on medium-low heat. When hot, add the honey. Once a full boil is reached, reduce the heat and simmer until the white tapioca pellets have turned clear.

• Remove from the heat. Cool on the counter. Cover with plastic wrap or waxed paper to keep a skin from forming. Cream the tofu in a blender. Fold the creamed tofu into the cooled pudding. Spoon the pudding into individual serving bowls, and refrigerate until firm.

Yield:
4 servings

Per serving:
Calories 172
Total Fat 1 g
Sat. Fat 0 g
Protein 4 g
Carb. 39 g
Fiber 2 g
Sodium 161 mg

❊ Coconut
Banana Cream Pie

This recipe looks more complicated than it is, and it's well worth the effort for a special occasion.

QUICK AND EASY OIL CRUST (single 9-inch)

⅛ teaspoon salt

1 cup whole wheat pastry flour

1 tablespoon soy flour

¼ cup oil

2 tablespoons cold soymilk or water

• Mix the salt into the flour in a mixing bowl. Pour the oil and milk or water into a cup without stirring. Pour onto the flour and mix with a fork or pastry blender. Form into a ball. Roll out the crust between two pieces of wax paper. Remove the top sheet of paper, and flip the crust over into a 9-inch pie pan. Remove the other paper.

• Prick the pie shell with a fork. Prebake the shell at 425°F for 10 to 12 minutes.

NOTE: *You may use the margarine crust recipe on page 130 or the Half-and-Half crust on page 132 (cut recipe in half); or use a crust recipe of your own.*

FILLING

½ cup unsweetened coconut

1½ cups soymilk or milk

1 cup water

4 large dates, chopped

½ teaspoon **powdered stevia extract**

1 teaspoon vanilla extract

3 tablespoons arrowroot powder or quick tapioca

• Grind the coconut to a powder in a dry blender. Set aside a few tablespoons to sprinkle on top of the pie. Soak the rest of the coconut in ½ cup of the soymilk or milk. Set aside. Bring ½ cup of the water to a boil on the stove or in the microwave. Remove from the heat and put in the chopped dates to soften. (This will make them easier to grind.) Soak both the dates and the coconut for about 10 minutes.

• Grind the softened dates and liquid in a food processor or blender until fairly smooth. Add the soaked coconut and liquid. Grind and process until creamy. Blend in the remaining cup of milk. Add the stevia extract, vanilla, and arrowroot powder or quick tapioca, and blend until mixed.

• Pour the mixture into a pan and cook while stirring over medium-low heat until thick. Simmer on low for 3 to 5 minutes more, stirring occasionally but gently. If using tapioca, let the mixture sit for 5 minutes in the pan without heat. Then gradually heat on medium to a full boil. Reduce the heat and cook, stirring about 5 minutes more or until the tapioca pellets look clear.

recipe continues on next page

BLENDED TOFU CREAM

8 ounces tofu

2 tablespoons oil

¼ teaspoon **stevia extract**

1 tablespoon honey or maple syrup (optional)

½ teaspoon vanilla

Pinch of salt

2 tablespoons agar–agar, or 1 package vegetarian gelatin

2 medium bananas, sliced

• Prepare 1 cup of tofu cream by blending the tofu, oil, stevia extract, honey or maple syrup, vanilla, and salt in a blender. Place the agar-agar and ½ cup water in a small saucepan. Bring to a boil, then simmer 3 to 4 minutes until dissolved. If using gelatin, soak the gelatin in ½ cup of cold water for 5 minutes in a pan. Heat on low until the gelatin is dissolved.

• Add the dissolved agar-agar or gelatin to the tofu cream in the blender by pouring it through the top while the blender is on low.

• Fold the tofu cream into the filling.

• Layer the sliced bananas in the bottom of the cooled, pre-baked pie shell. If preferred, half of the bananas may be mashed and folded into the filling. Pour the filling over the bananas in the pie shell. Dust the top of the pie with powdered coconut. Chill in the refrigerator at least 4 hours.

NOTES: *If agar-agar is unavailable, use an extra tablespoon of arrowroot powder or quick tapioca. However, the agar gives a creamier, lighter filling with a better shape.*

If using dairy whipped cream, beat it with ¼ teaspoon stevia extract. Gently stir the dissolved agar into the filling, then fold in the whipped cream after the filling has cooled some.

Yield:
8 servings

Per serving:
Calories 365
Total Fat 24 g
Sat. Fat 9 g
Protein 7 g
Carb. 32 g
Fiber 7 g
Sodium 84 mg

✤ PEAR CUSTARD PIE

FILLING

2½ to 3 cups fresh or canned, drained sliced pears

1¼ cups low-fat cottage cheese

⅓ cup soymilk or milk

1 large egg

1 teaspoon vanilla extract

½ teaspoon **powdered stevia extract**

2 tablespoons flour

Pinch of salt

• Preheat the oven to 350°F. Prepare a 9-inch single pie crust (see page 120, 130, or 132; or use your own recipe). Prick the crust with a fork a number of times, and bake for 15 minutes. Remove from the oven.

• Lay the pear slices in the pie shell. Blend the remaining ingredients together in a blender until smooth. Pour the blended mixture over the pears. Bake for 30 to 40 minutes. Remove from the oven.

TOPPING

½ cup whole wheat flour

1 teaspoon cinnamon

1 tablespoon butter

¾ teaspoon **stevia concentrate**

• Raise the oven temperature to 400°F.

• Place the flour in a small bowl. Stir in the cinnamon. Mix in the butter then the stevia concentrate until well distributed. Sprinkle evenly over the top of the pie. Return to the oven and bake for 10 to 15 minutes longer.

• Chill before serving.

Yield:
8 servings

Per serving:
Calories 268
Total Fat 11 g
Sat. Fat 3 g
Protein 10 g
Carb. 32 g
Fiber 5 g
Sodium 286 mg

Strawberry Cream Pie

GRANOLA CRUST (single 9-inch)

1⅓ cups granola

3 tablespoons oil

2 tablespoons apple juice or water

• Preheat the oven to 300°F.

• Grind the granola in a blender until fine. Place in a bowl and lightly stir in the oil with a fork. Sprinkle and stir in the juice or water.

• Press the mixture into the bottom and sides of a 9-inch pie pan. Bake for 15 minutes. Chill before filling.

NOTE: *You may use the Crumb Crust recipe, page 58, or the Nut and Seed Crust recipe, page 126, or use one of your own.*

FILLING

1 cup whipped cream

4 cups fresh strawberries, or about 3½ cups (one 1-pound bag) sliced frozen strawberries, thawed

2 tablespoons honey, warmed (optional)

¾ teaspoon **powdered stevia extract**

Pinch of salt

2½ tablespoons agar-agar, or 1 package vegetarian gelatin

½ cup apple juice

1 large banana, sliced

• Have ready 1 cup of whipped cream. Use whipped dairy cream or Tofu "Whipped Cream" (page 165). If whipping dairy cream, beat in ¼ teaspoon stevia extract.

- Slice the strawberries and put aside 1 cup. Crush the rest in a bowl, and stir in the warmed honey, ½ teaspoon stevia extract, and salt.

- Place the agar-agar and apple juice in a small pan. Bring to a boil then simmer over medium heat for 3 to 4 minutes until dissolved. If using gelatin, soak the gelatin in the cold juice for 5 minutes in a small pan, then simmer until completely dissolved. Mix into the crushed berries.

- Fold the cup of whipped cream into the agar filling. Put a layer of sliced strawberries in the bottom of the cooled pie shell. Put a layer of sliced bananas on top of the strawberries. Follow with another layer of sliced strawberries. Pour the filling into the pie pan. Chill for 4 hours or longer.

OPTION: *For a creamy filling, blend 3 cups of sliced strawberries in the blender first with the sweeteners and salt. Blend in the dissolved agar or gelatin by pouring through the top of the blender in a stream while the blender is on. Transfer to a large bowl, and fold in the whipped cream. If using blended strawberries and tofu whipped cream, the entire filling can be made in the blender. You may need an extra tablespoon of agar or ½ package vegetarian gelatin. Layer with the remaining strawberries and bananas as above.*

NOTE: *If using frozen berries omit the layering in the bottom of the pie shell or layer first with bananas followed by one layer of thawed strawberry slices (to prevent a soggy crust). Slice and thaw a 1-pound bag of frozen berries and follow the directions above. Use a total of 3½ tablespoons agar-agar or 1½ packages of vegetarian gelatin.*

Yield:
8 servings

Per serving:
Calories 240
Total Fat 14 g
Sat. Fat 4 g
Protein 3 g
Carb. 28 g
Fiber 4 g
Sodium 66 mg

BLACKBERRY CREAM PIE

NUT AND SEED CRUST (single 9-inch)

½ cup chopped figs or raisins

½ cup chopped dates

2 tablespoons apple juice or water

¼ cup unsweetened coconut

½ cup raw sesame seeds

¼ cup raw sunflower seeds

⅓ cup raw almonds

• Toasting the crust is optional. Preheat the oven to 300°F if you wish to toast it first.

• Place the fruit in a small saucepan with the apple juice or water, and soften over low heat for a few minutes.

• Grind the coconut, seeds, and nuts to a fine meal in a blender or food processor. Place in a bowl and mix in the stewed fruit. Grind the mixture in the blender or food processor. If using a blender, place about ⅓ of the mixture at a time in the blender. Use the pulse button, stirring between pulses. When blended and ground, remove and put in another portion to grind.

• Press the mixture into the bottom and sides of a 9-inch pie pan. Bake for 15 minutes, if desired. If baked, cool before filling. If unbaked, chill in the refrigerator before filling.

NOTE: *You may use any combination of nuts, seeds, and dried fruit for the crust. You may also use the Crumb Crust, page 58 or the Granola Crust, page 124, if preferred.*

FILLING

4 cups fresh or frozen ripe blackberries

1 cup water

1 cup unsweetened apple juice

2 tablespoons lemon juice

Pinch of salt

1 (12.3-ounce) box firm silken tofu

1 teaspoon vanilla extract

¾ teaspoon **powdered stevia extract**

3 tablespoons agar–agar, or 1½ packages vegetarian gelatin

• To make the filling, cook the blackberries in the water, apple juice, lemon juice, and salt until the fruit is completely broken down. After cooking, press the berries through a fine-mesh strainer to remove the seeds. You should have 2 cups of berry sauce. If you have more, boil it down until you only have 2 cups.

• Frozen berries may be used, but cut back on the cooking liquid from 2 cups to about 1¾ cups. As above, end up with 2 cups of berry sauce.

recipe continues on next page

- Blend the tofu, vanilla, and stevia extract in a blender or food processor until creamy with 1 cup of the berry sauce.
- Place the other cup of berry sauce in a small pan. Dissolve the agar-agar in the hot sauce. Bring to a boil and reduce to a simmer, cooking until dissolved (about 3 to 4 minutes), stirring occasionally.
- If using gelatin, use ½ cup of the cold water from the ingredients list to soak the gelatin for several minutes. Mix it into the hot berry sauce, and stir until dissolved. Don't add an extra ½ cup of liquid.
- Add the berry sauce with the dissolved agar-agar or gelatin to the mixture in the blender or processor, and mix until smooth.
- Pour the contents into the cooled pie shell. Chill for 2 hours or more.

OPTION: *Serve topped with "Whipped Cream" (see page 164 or 165), or use dairy whipped cream.*

Yield:
8 servings

Per serving:
Calories 335
Total Fat 19 g
Sat. Fat 6 g
Protein 12 g
Carb. 36 g
Fiber 11 g
Sodium 30 mg

TOFU PUMPKIN PIE

FILLING

1 (12.3-ounce) box silken tofu, soft or firm

⅓ cup oil

2 packed cups cooked, fresh pumpkin or 1 (15-ounce) can plain pumpkin

2 tablespoons maple syrup (optional)

2 tablespoons date sugar (optional)

½ teaspoon maple flavoring

¾ teaspoon **powdered stevia extract**

½ teaspoon salt

1 teaspoon cinnamon

½ teaspoon ginger

¼ teaspoon nutmeg

⅛ teaspoon cloves

• Prepare a single 9-inch crust. Use one of the recipes on pages 120, 130, or 132; or use one of your own.

• Preheat the oven to 350°F.

• Blend all the ingredients for the filling until smooth and creamy in a blender or food processor. If using a blender, start with some of the tofu and the oil. Gradually add the rest of the ingredients. Use the pulse button, stirring in between pulses.

• Pour into an unbaked pie shell. You may partially bake the pie shell for 15 minutes at 350°F before adding the filling. Bake for 45 minutes to 1 hour. Chill and serve topped with "Whipped Cream" (see page 164 or 165), or use dairy whipped cream.

Yield:
8 servings

Per serving:
Calories 259
Total Fat 19 g
Sat. Fat 3 g
Protein 7 g
Carb. 18 g
Fiber 4 g
Sodium 254 mg

✳ TRADITIONAL PUMPKIN PIE

A basic recipe that can be made with sweet potatoes, squash, yams, or pumpkin

MARGARINE CRUST (single 9-inch)

⅛ teaspoon salt

1 cup whole wheat pastry flour

2 tablespoons soy flour

5 tablespoons soy or canola margarine, softened

2 to 3 tablespoons cold water

• Mix the salt into the flours in a mixing bowl. Cut the margarine into the flour with a pastry blender or fork until it is well distributed and the dough looks like a coarse meal. Sprinkle the water in gradually while mixing the flour. Start with 2 tablespoons; if still dry add more water.

• Form into a ball and roll out between two pieces of wax paper or use a floured board and rolling pin. Remove the top sheet of paper and flip the crust over into a pie pan. Remove the other paper, and trim and flute edges. You may also use the oil crust on page 120 or the Half-and-Half crust on page 132.

• Preheat the oven to 350°F. Partially bake the crust for 15 minutes. Remove from the oven and cool.

FILLING

1 teaspoon cinnamon

½ teaspoon ginger

¼ teaspoon nutmeg

⅛ teaspoon cloves

¼ teaspoon salt

1 tablespoon date sugar (optional)

¾ teaspoon **powdered stevia extract**

2 packed cups cooked, fresh pumpkin or
    1 (15-ounce) can plain pumpkin

½ teaspoon vanilla extract

2 tablespoons maple syrup (optional)

1½ cups soymilk or milk

2 eggs

• Mix the spices, salt, date sugar, and stevia extract into the pumpkin in a large bowl. Stir in the vanilla, maple syrup, and soymilk or milk. Lightly beat the eggs in a small bowl. Mix well into the pumpkin.

• Place the filling in the pie shell. Bake for 45 to 50 minutes or until a knife inserted at the edge of the pie comes out clean.

NOTES: *Make sure the eggs are well mixed into the pumpkin.*

The filling may be made in a blender. Place all the ingredients in a blender, and process until smooth. However, the top surface of the pie may have a rough appearance.

Yield:
8 servings

Per serving:
Calories 191
Total Fat 10 g
Sat. Fat 2 g
Protein 7 g
Carb. 19 g
Fiber 4 g
Sodium 206 mg

❧ Deep Dish Apple Pie

HALF-AND-HALF CRUST
(Double Crust)

¼ teaspoon salt

1 cup whole wheat pastry flour

1 cup unbleached white flour

2 tablespoons soy flour

6 tablespoons cold butter

6 tablespoons cold oil

4 to 6 tablespoons ice water

• Mix the salt into the flours. Cut the butter up into pieces and lay over the flour in a bowl. Mix the butter into the flour with a pastry blender or fork until well distributed. Gradually add the oil and mix until the dough looks like a coarse meal. Sprinkle in 4 tablespoons of water, and mix until the dough can be gathered into a ball. If the dough is still dry, add another tablespoon of water and another if needed. Wrap the dough in waxed paper, and chill for 20 to 30 minutes in the refrigerator. This keeps the dough from shrinking so much in the oven.

• Break the dough into two parts with one part a little larger than the other. Use the smaller part for the bottom crust. Roll the dough out on a lightly floured board with a floured rolling pin. Flip the dough over several times as the dough is being rolled out and re-flour the board. Fold the rolled-out dough in half and place in a 9½-inch deep-dish pie pan. Trim to the edge of the pan. Use the larger portion of dough for the top crust. Either extend the top edge over the pie pan and fold it under the bottom edge and flute or have the top crust just come to the edge of the pie pan, and use a fork to press both edges together. Score the top crust for steam holes.

FILLING

8 to 9 cups sliced apples (8 to 10 large apples, or enough to form a heaping mound in the pie pan)

1½ tablespoons lemon juice

¼ cup apple juice concentrate or blend, thawed

1 teaspoon **powdered stevia extract**

1 tablespoon arrowroot powder

2 tablespoons wheat flour

1 teaspoon cinnamon

¼ teaspoon nutmeg

2 tablespoons date sugar

¼ teaspoon salt

2 tablespoons butter or margarine (optional)

• Peel, core, and slice the apples into a large bowl. Mix the lemon juice into the apples well, then stir in the apple juice concentrate and stevia extract. Cover the bowl and refrigerate for several hours to overnight.

• Preheat the oven to 425°F.

• Roll out the bottom crust. Mix the arrowroot, flour, spices, date sugar, and salt together in a small bowl. Stir the dry ingredients into the apples, coating every piece. Place the apples in an uncooked pie shell. Cut up the butter or margarine and place pieces on top of the apples.

• Roll out the top crust. Place over the pie and cut in steam holes. Bake at 425°F for 10 minutes. Reduce the temperature to 350°F and bake for 35 to 45 minutes longer. The apple pieces should be tender. Poke with a fork through the steam holes.

NOTES: *Most apple pie recipes call for tart apples. Since there is very little sugar in this recipe I use a sweeter apple.*

If using a regular-size pie pan, cut down on all the ingredients in the recipe.

Yield:
8 servings

Per serving:
Calories 414
Total Fat 21 g
Sat. Fat 7 g
Protein 5 g
Carb. 54 g
Fiber 21 g
Sodium 229 mg

❧ LEMON MERINGUE PIE

FILLING

3 egg yolks

Juice of 2 lemons (4 ounces)

Finely grated rind of 2 lemons

6 tablespoons cornstarch

1 cup water

1½ cups soymilk or milk

4 tablespoons honey or maple syrup (optional)

1 teaspoon **powdered stevia extract**

Pinch of salt

• Prepare a single 9-inch pie shell. See page 120, 130, or 132 for recipes, or use one of your own. Prick pie shell with a fork and bake at 425°F for 10 to 12 minutes.

• Reduce the oven temperature to 350°F.

• Separate the egg yolks from the whites, and put aside. Save the whites for the meringue.

• Juice the lemons and grate the rind into a small bowl. Put aside.

• Dissolve the cornstarch in ½ cup of the water in a cup or small bowl. Heat the rest of the water and the milk in a heavy-bottomed saucepan or double boiler. Stir in the honey or maple syrup, stevia extract, and salt. When hot but not boiling, slowly mix in the cornstarch. Cook on low, stirring gently until thick (about 5 minutes). Simmer for about 3 to 5 minutes longer on low.

• Mix the egg yolks, lemon juice, and rind together. Gradually mix about 1 cup of the hot pudding into the eggs. Add the egg mixture slowly back into the pan. Cook for 3 to 5 minutes longer on low, stirring gently.

- Remove the pudding from the heat. Cool to a warm temperature. To prevent a skin from forming, place a piece of waxed paper on the surface.
- Place the filling in the pre-baked pie shell. Top with the meringue.

MERINGUE

3 egg whites

¼ teaspoon cream of tartar

1 teaspoon honey (optional)

½ teaspoon vanilla extract

Pinch of **powdered stevia extract**

- Beat the egg whites with a mixer until frothy at medium speed. Add the cream of tartar.
- Whip on medium-high until the whites form soft peaks that droop. Drizzle in the honey, then add the vanilla and stevia extract.

- Continue beating on medium-high until the whites are smooth, moist, and shiny, and when the beater is lifted the meringue stands in straight peaks.
- Spread the meringue on the pie, making sure it goes all the way to the edge. Form peaks with a knife if desired.
- Bake in a 350°F oven for 15 to 18 minutes. If the peaks are getting too dark, take the pie out of the oven early. Next time, try lowering the oven temperature slightly or lower the oven rack.

Yield:
8 servings

Per serving:
Calories 198
Total Fat 11 g
Sat. Fat 2 g
Protein 7 g
Carb. 19 g
Fiber 3 g
Sodium 157 mg

❊ APPLE CRISP

FILLING

7 to 8 cups chopped apples (peeling is optional)

3 tablespoons lemon juice

1 teaspoon vanilla

1 to 1½ teaspoons **powdered stevia leaf** or
  ½ teaspoon **powdered stevia extract**

2 tablespoons whole wheat flour

3 tablespoons natural peanut butter (optional)

1 teaspoon cinnamon

¼ teaspoon salt

⅔ cup apple juice or blend

TOPPING

1 cup rolled oats

⅔ cup chopped nuts and seeds

¼ teaspoon **powdered stevia extract**

¾ teaspoon **stevia concentrate**

2 tablespoons oil

Yield:
8 servings

Per serving:
Calories 228
Total Fat 11 g
Sat. Fat 1 g
Protein 4 g
Carb. 33 g
Fiber 5 g
Sodium 69 mg

• Preheat the oven to 350°F. Butter a large, 9 x 13-inch baking dish.

• Place the apples in a large mixing bowl. Stir in the lemon juice. Mix the vanilla, stevia leaf or stevia extract, flour, peanut butter, cinnamon, and salt into the apples.

• Pour the fruit juice into the bottom of the dish. Spoon in the apple mixture.

• Mix the oats, chopped nuts and seeds, stevia extract, and stevia concentrate together in a bowl. Sprinkle and stir in the oil. Spread the topping over the apples so it is evenly distributed.

• Bake for 50 minutes to 1 hour. If the topping gets done before the apples, cover pan with foil the last 15 minutes of baking

OPTION: *Use about 1½ cups granola for the topping. Mix ½ cup of the granola into the apples, and spread the rest on the top. No need to add the stevia extract, stevia concentrate, and oil from topping recipe above—granola already has sweetener and oil.*

 # PEACH CRUMBLE

FILLING

8 to 10 fresh ripe peaches

½ teaspoon **powdered stevia extract**

2 tablespoons date sugar (optional)

¼ cup unsweetened fruit juice

2 tablespoons arrowroot powder

1 teaspoon cinnamon

1 teaspoon vanilla extract

Pinch of salt

• Preheat the oven to 375°F. Butter the bottom and sides of a 9 x 13-inch glass baking pan.

• Peel and slice the peaches into a mixing bowl. Mix in the stevia extract, date sugar, fruit juice, arrowroot, cinnamon, vanilla, and salt, coating the peaches. Lay the peaches out in the bottom of the baking pan.

TOPPING

1 cup whole wheat flour

¼ teaspoon salt

¼ teaspoon **powdered stevia extract** or
  ½ teaspoon **stevia concentrate**

¼ teaspoon cinnamon

2 tablespoons oil

2 tablespoons maple syrup (optional)

• Combine the flour, salt, stevia extract, and cinnamon in a bowl. Lightly cut in the oil using a fork or your fingers. Rub in the maple syrup until well distributed. (If using stevia concentrate, blend it in with the maple syrup.) Crumble the mixture over the peaches.

• Bake for 40 to 45 minutes. If the top is getting too brown, cover the pan with foil during the last 15 to 20 minutes of baking.

VARIATION: *For part of the flour use wheat germ or ground sesame seeds.*

Yield:
8 servings

Per serving:
Calories 144
Total Fat 4 g
Sat. Fat 0 g
Protein 3 g
Carb. 25 g
Fiber 4 g
Sodium 81 mg

❧ BLUEBERRY PIE

• Prepare a double crust. Use the Half-and-Half crust recipe on page 132 or double one of the recipes on page 120 or 130, or use your own recipe. The top crust may be whole or latticed.

> 4 cups fresh or frozen blueberries
>
> 4 tablespoons quick tapioca
>
> 2 tablespoons date sugar (optional)
>
> ¾ teaspoon **powdered stevia extract**
>
> 1 tablespoon lemon juice
>
> 1 tablespoon butter

• Preheat the oven to 450°F.

• If using frozen berries, take them out to thaw before making the crust. They just have to be thawed enough so they're not clumped together.

• In a bowl, mix the berries with the rest of the ingredients except the butter. Let the berry mixture set for 15 minutes.

• Place the berries in the unbaked pie shell. Dot the top with pieces of butter. Roll out the top crust. Cut for a latticed top or use whole with vents. Flute the edge.

• Bake at 450°F for 10 minutes. Reduce the heat to 350°F, and bake for 45 minutes to 1 hour until golden brown.

Yield:
8 servings

Per serving:
Calories 345
Total Fat 22 g
Sat. Fat 7 g
Protein 5 g
Carb. 33 g
Fiber 5 g
Sodium 179 mg

Simply Fruit and Gelatin Desserts

 # BAKED PEARS

A simple way to enjoy this seasonal fruit

10 to 12 pears

1 cup fruit juice

1 tablespoon cornstarch or arrowroot powder

2 tablespoons lemon juice

1 teaspoon cinnamon

½ teaspoon **powdered stevia extract**

• Preheat the oven to 350°F.

• Peel, core, and quarter the pears. Place 8 to 10 of the quartered pears in a large baking dish (approximately 9 x 13 inches).

• Place the remaining pears in a blender with the rest of the ingredients. Blend until smooth. Pour the mixture over the pears in the baking dish.

• Bake covered about 1 hour until the pears are tender. Pears vary greatly in hardness, and some types may take a long time to soften.

Yield:
10 servings

Per serving:
Calories 123
Total Fat 1 g
Sat. Fat 0 g
Protein 1 g
Carb. 31 g
Fiber 5 g
Sodium 1 mg

❧ SUMMER FRUIT SALAD

Stevia really makes a fruit salad come alive! Use the fruit suggested below or your favorite combination.

2 cups melon chunks or balls (about ½ melon)
1 cup blueberries or other fresh berries
2 large bananas, sliced
2 ripe peaches or nectarines
1 cup halved cherries or grapes

• Cut up the fruit and place in a large bowl. Dress with one of the following dressings, and chill in the refrigerator before serving.

Yield:
8 servings

Per serving:
w/ Dressing 1
Calories 87
Total Fat 1 g
Sat. Fat 0 g
Protein 1 g
Carb. 22 g
Fiber 2 g
Sodium 5 mg

Per serving:
w/ Dressing 2
Calories 90
Total Fat 1 g
Sat. Fat 0 g
Protein 3 g
Carb. 2 g
Fiber 2 g
Sodium 29 mg

DRESSING 1

*Mix together and stir into
    the fruit:*

¼ cup unsweetened frozen
    orange juice concentrate
    or orange blend, thawed
1 tablespoon lemon juice
⅓ to ½ teaspoon **powdered
    stevia extract**

DRESSING 2

*Mix together and stir into
    the fruit:*

1 cup low-fat yogurt
1 teaspoon vanilla extract
⅓ to ½ teaspoon **powdered
    stevia extract**

𝕬 FRUIT COMPOTE

1 tablespoon mulling spices*

2 to 3 **stevia tea bags**

1½ cups water

2 cups fresh fruit of choice, diced or halved if
using grapes and/or cherries

• Simmer the spices and stevia tea bags in the water for about
10 to 15 minutes. Remove the spices and stevia. Return the
water to the heat and bring to a boil. Drop the fruit into the
liquid, and immediately reduce to a simmer. Simmer about 1
minute or until the fruit is tender. Serve immediately in the
sweet, spicy sauce.

• Very soft fruit like ripe peaches or ripe pears will need to be
quickly cooled down by placing the pan in a cold water bath
to keep the fruit from overcooking. Hard fruit like apples will
have to be cooked longer than the other fruit.

*Suggested fruit: pears, peaches, kiwi, cherries, grapes, or
blueberries.*

*To make your own spice mix, use:

1 teaspoon whole cloves

1 teaspoon whole allspice

1 cinnamon stick

Yield:
4 servings

Per serving:
Calories 85
Total Fat 1 g
Sat. Fat 0 g
Protein 1 g
Carb. 22 g
Fiber 5 g
Sodium 1 mg

# APPLE MOUSSE

3 cups unsweetened, filtered apple juice

3 tablespoons agar-agar, or 1½ packages vegetarian gelatin

⅓ teaspoon **powdered stevia extract**

1 teaspoon vanilla extract

1½ to 2 tablespoons cashew butter or sesame tahini

• Combine the juice and agar-agar in a small pan. Bring to a boil then reduce to a simmer. Simmer for 4 to 5 minutes, stirring until the agar is dissolved. Remove from the heat and stir in the stevia extract and vanilla.

• Pour into a shallow dish, and chill several hours until set.

• Remove from the refrigerator. Break up the agar with a spatula, and place it in a blender or food processor. Puree on low speed until creamy. Blend in the cashew butter or tahini. Spoon into custard cups and serve immediately.

NOTE: *This dessert is best if you use agar. If using gelatin, sprinkle the gelatin over ½ cup cold juice in a wide bowl. Let soften for several minutes. Heat the rest of the juice to the boiling point and pour into the gelatin. Stir until the gelatin is dissolved, about 3 to 5 minutes. Mix in the stevia extract. Refrigerate until set. Remove from the refrigerator. Break up the gelatin and place in a blender. Blend with the nut butter until smooth. Serve immediately or return to the refrigerator to re-set.*

Yield:
4 servings

Per serving:
Calories 136
Total Fat 4 g
Sat. Fat 1 g
Protein 1 g
Carb. 25 g
Fiber 2 g
Sodium 14 mg

CRANBERRY GELATIN SALAD

½ cup grapes, cut in half

¾ cup chopped, unpeeled red apples

1 tablespoon lemon juice

½ cup chopped cranberries

¾ teaspoon **powdered stevia extract**

¼ cup chopped walnuts (optional)

12 ounces frozen unsweetened cran-apple juice concentrate, thawed

2½ cups water

2 packages vegetarian gelatin, or 4 tablespoons agar-agar

• Sprinkle the grapes and apples with the lemon juice, and set aside. Chop the cranberries in a blender or food processor. Mix some of the stevia extract into the cranberries. Set aside. Chop the nuts and set aside.

• Place ½ cup of the juice concentrate and ½ cup of water in a pan. Sprinkle the gelatin on top. Let the gelatin soften for about 3 minutes. Simmer on low until the gelatin is dissolved. Mix in the rest of the stevia extract.

• In a bowl, mix together the rest of the juice concentrate and water. Add the gelatin. Place the bowl in the refrigerator until the gelatin is partly set (the consistency of egg whites).

• When the gelatin is partly set, mix in the fruit and nuts. Spoon into individual serving bowls or into a single mold, and return to the refrigerator to re-set.

NOTE: *If you are using agar-agar, heat 1 cup of water in a pan. Add the agar and bring to a boil. Reduce the heat and simmer for about 5 minutes until the agar is completely dissolved. In a separate bowl, mix the dissolved agar into the*

Yield:
8 servings

Per serving:
Calories 116
Total Fat 3 g
Sat. Fat 0 g
Protein 1 g
Carb. 23 g
Fiber 2 g
Sodium 16 mg

juice concentrate and the rest of the water. Stir in the stevia extract. Place the fruit and nuts in a dish and pour the juice mixture over them. Chill in the refrigerator for several hours.

SPARKLING GELATIN

12 ounces unsweetened frozen apple-raspberry juice
　concentrate, thawed

½ cup water

2 packages vegetarian gelatin

½ teaspoon **powdered stevia extract**

2 cups sparkling water

2 cups raspberries

Yield:
8 servings

Per serving:
Calories 92
Total Fat 0 g
Sat. Fat 0 g
Protein 2 g
Carb. 21 g
Fiber 2 g
Sodium 14 mg

• Place ½ cup of the juice concentrate and the water in a small pan. Sprinkle the gelatin over the surface. Let stand for 5 minutes. Cook on low until the gelatin is dissolved. Mix in the stevia extract.

• In a bowl, add the rest of the juice concentrate, the sparkling water, and the dissolved gelatin. Refrigerate until partly set (the consistency of egg whites). Stir in the berries. Pour into a mold or individual serving bowls. Return to the refrigerator until firmly set.

NOTE: *Agar doesn't set well when using sparkling water.*

Fruit Juice Gelatin

4 cups filtered, unsweetened fruit juice

4 tablespoons agar-agar, or 2 packages vegetarian gelatin

½ teaspoon **powdered stevia extract**

1 cup fruit (optional)

• Place 1 cup of juice in a saucepan with the agar. Bring the juice to a boil and then reduce to a simmer. Simmer 4 to 5 minutes until the agar is dissolved. Mix in the stevia extract and the rest of the juice.

• Place fresh, frozen, or canned (drained) fruit into the bottom of a dish or mold. You may use bananas, berries, pears, or peaches. Pour the juice mixture over the fruit. Refrigerate until set.

Suggested juices: apple or white grape juice blend with raspberry or strawberry, peach or pear blends.

VARIATION: *Break up the plain fruit juice gelatin and place in a blender. Blend with 1 to 2 cups of whipped cream until creamy. Serve immediately.*

NOTE: *If using gelatin, sprinkle it over 1 cup cold juice in a wide bowl, and let it soften for several minutes. Heat the rest of the juice to boiling in a pan, and pour over the gelatin in the bowl. Stir for about 3 to 5 minutes until the gelatin is dissolved. Mix in the stevia extract. If adding fruit, refrigerate the gelatin first until it reaches the consistency of egg whites (about 1 hour). Remove from the refrigerator and add fruit, or blend in whipped cream and then add fruit. Return to the refrigerator until set.*

Yield:
8 servings

Per serving:
Calories 63
Total Fat 0 g
Sat. Fat 0 g
Protein 0 g
Carb. 15 g
Fiber 1 g
Sodium 9 mg

Sauces and Toppings

 # APPLESAUCE

METHOD I

    6 cups peeled, cored, and chopped apples

    3 cups water

    1½ teaspoons cinnamon

    ¾ teaspoon **powdered stevia extract**

    ½ teaspoon **stevia concentrate** (optional)

• Blend the apples and water together in a blender, 2 cups of apples to 1 cup of water at a time. Pour into a saucepan and cook over medium-low heat. Add the cinnamon, stevia extract, and stevia concentrate, if desired. Cook until heated through and the sauce reaches the desired thickness.

METHOD II

    8 to 10 cups chopped apples

    1½ teaspoons cinnamon

    ¾ teaspoon **powdered stevia extract**

    ½ teaspoon **stevia concentrate** (optional)

• Don't peel or core the apples, but cut out any bad spots. Cover the apples with water in a large pot. Boil down the apples for about 45 minutes to an hour. Stir occasionally and add more water if necessary. Cook until the apples are completely softened.

• Remove from the heat and push the apples through a sieve or strainer. Keep pressing until only the peels and cores are

Yield:
About 1 quart
(8 servings)

Per serving:
(either method)
Calories 49
Total Fat 0 g
Sat. Fat 0 g
Protein 0 g
Carb. 13 g
Fiber 2 g
Sodium 0 mg

left. Return to the pan and stir in the cinnamon, stevia extract, and stevia concentrate, if using.

• If canning follow standard procedures. Sterilize the jars and lids. Return the sauce to a boil. Pour the sauce into the jars and cover.

APPLE BUTTER

1 quart unsweetened applesauce
Apple juice
Cinnamon to taste (about 1½ teaspoons)
Powdered stevia extract to taste (about ½ teaspoon)
½ teaspoon **stevia concentrate** (optional)

• Pour the applesauce into a heavy-bottomed pan. (If using homemade sauce, use method II on page 150.)

• Boil the applesauce on low for several hours, stirring occasionally. Periodically adding some apple juice or cider will make the apple butter creamier and richer, but it will take longer to thicken.

• Add cinnamon, stevia extract, and stevia concentrate, if using, to taste. Cook until the applesauce is reduced in half or more or until the desired thickness is reached.

NOTE: *If your applesauce is already sweetened with stevia extract and concentrate, you will probably not need to add all of the stevia called for in this recipe.*

Yield:
8 servings

Per serving:
Calories 49
Total Fat 0 g
Sat. Fat 0 g
Protein 0 g
Carb. 13 g
Fiber 2 g
Sodium 0 mg

☙ FRUIT JUICE SAUCE

1 cup fruit juice

1½ tablespoons arrowroot powder or cornstarch

⅛ to ¼ teaspoon **powdered stevia extract**

1 teaspoon lemon juice or
    ½ teaspoon vanilla extract (optional)

1 teaspoon honey (optional)

• Whip the fruit juice and arrowroot powder or cornstarch together with the stevia extract in a small heavy-bottomed pan.

• Cook on medium heat until the sauce reaches a boil. Simmer for several minutes longer on low (5 minutes if using cornstarch).

• Remove from the heat. The sauce may be enhanced by adding a mixture of lemon juice and honey, or vanilla extract and honey, depending on the juice used. Try it and decide what tastes best. Serve warm over cake, custard, or tarts.

These juices work well: pineapple, pineapple/coconut blend, peach or pear puree, mango or papaya blends.

Yield:
4 servings

Per serving:
Calories 41
Total Fat 0 g
Sat. Fat 0 g
Protein 0 g
Carb. 10 g
Fiber <1 g
Sodium 2 mg

PLUM SAUCE

2 cups pitted, chopped plums
Water to cover
¼ to ⅓ teaspoon **powdered stevia extract**

• Chop the plums and remove the pits. Place them in a saucepan, and cover with water. Cook about 1 hour until soft.

• Once the plums are completely softened, remove them from the heat, and strain them through a sieve or strainer. Return to the pan. Add the stevia extract and cook the sauce until it reaches the desired thickness.

NOTES: *Some plums are hard and will take a lot longer to cook than soft ones. Both hard and soft plums work well making a wonderfully rich red sauce.*

For pouring over pancakes, etc., use a thinner sauce. For spreading the sauce on toast or for filling crepes, make a thicker sauce.

Yield:
4 servings

Per serving:
Calories 45
Total Fat 1 g
Sat. Fat 0 g
Protein 1 g
Carb. 11 g
Fiber 1 g
Sodium 0 mg

❧ CREAMY CRANBERRY SAUCE

1 (12-ounce) package cranberries (about 4 cups)
1½ cups unsweetened apple juice
½ cup orange juice
3 to 4 tablespoons maple syrup or honey
¾ to 1 teaspoon **powdered stevia extract**
Finely grated rind of 1 orange

• Pick out and discard any soft berries. If there are a lot of soft berries to be discarded, reduce the apple juice and sweeteners accordingly. Place the berries in a saucepan with the apple juice. Cook over medium heat for about 30 minutes until the berries are mostly broken down.

• Add the orange juice, maple syrup or honey, and stevia extract. Cook over low heat for about 30 more minutes, stirring occasionally.

• When the sauce is getting thick and creamy, remove it from the heat and put it through a fine-mesh strainer. Return it to the pan, add the finely grated orange rind, and cook for 20 to 30 minutes more on low, stirring occasionally.

• Cool on the counter then refrigerate. Cranberry sauce thickens upon cooling.

see variation next page

Yield:
6 servings
(about
1½ cups)

Per serving:
Calories 97
Total Fat 0 g
Sat. Fat 0 g
Protein 0 g
Carb. 24 g
Fiber 2 g
Sodium 4 mg

VARIATION: *For a whole cranberry sauce, place the cranberries in the apple juice in a saucepan, and cook on medium for about 10 minutes until the skins burst. Mix in the stevia extract, maple syrup or honey, orange juice, and grated orange peel. Simmer about 5 to 10 minutes longer until the sauce starts to thicken. Cool on a counter then refrigerate.*

APRICOT SAUCE

1 cup dried apricots

Enough unsweetened apple juice to cover plus 1 cup

1 teaspoon **stevia concentrate** or
   ½ teaspoon **powdered stevia extract**

1 tablespoon arrowroot powder

Pinch of salt

Yield:
4 servings

Per serving:
Calories 116
Total Fat 0 g
Sat. Fat 0 g
Protein 1 g
Carb. 28 g
Fiber 3 g
Sodium 32 mg

• Simmer the apricots in the juice until very tender, about 45 minutes. Periodically add more juice as necessary to keep the apricots covered.

• Place the cooked apricots in a blender with the cup of apple juice, stevia concentrate or stevia extract, arrowroot, and salt. Process until smooth. Add a little extra juice if the apricots are still too thick to blend. Return to the pan and cook over low heat for several minutes until thickened. Serve warm or cold.

BERRY SAUCE

1 cup fresh or frozen unsweetened berries

½ cup unsweetened apple juice or apple blend

2 teaspoons lemon juice

⅓ to ½ teaspoon **powdered stevia extract** (to taste)

1 tablespoon quick tapioca or arrowroot powder

• Blend the berries, apple juice, and lemon juice together in a blender. To remove the seeds, pass through a fine-mesh strainer. Pour into a saucepan. Whisk in the stevia extract and quick tapioca or arrowroot powder.

• If using tapioca, let the ingredients sit in the pan with no heat for 15 minutes. Cook over medium heat until a full boil is reached. Cook until the tapioca turns clear, and remove from the heat. It will thicken as it cools.

• If using arrowroot powder, heat on low, stirring gently until the sauce is thick. Remove from heat when it reaches the boiling point. It will get thicker as it cools.

SERVING SUGGESTIONS: *Serve warmed over pancakes and waffles, or use as an ice cream topping. For a pourable syrup, use a little less thickener. To use as a filling, for crepes or layer cakes, make the sauce a little thicker. It will keep for several weeks in a covered container in the refrigerator.*

OPTION: *If you prefer a whole berry sauce, eliminate the step of pureeing the fruit in the blender. Just whisk the thickener into the berries and liquid.*

Yield:
1 cup (6
servings)

Per serving:
Calories 29
Total Fat 0 g
Sat. Fat 0 g
Protein 0 g
Carb. 7 g
Fiber 0.7 g
Sodium 2 mg

# CHOCOLATE SAUCE

1 teaspoon **powdered stevia extract**

6 level tablespoons cocoa

1 cup soymilk or milk

4 tablespoons honey

1 teaspoon vanilla extract

1 tablespoon butter

• In a small pan, stir the stevia extract into the cocoa. Cream in about half of the soymilk or milk. Bring to a light boil. Add the honey. Gradually stir in the rest of the milk while the mixture is boiling. Boil for 2 to 3 minutes. Remove from heat. Beat in the vanilla and butter.

• Serve warm or cold over ice cream.

Yield:
about 1 cup
(4 servings)

Per serving:
Calories 75
Total Fat 5 g
Sat. Fat 0 g
Protein 4 g
Carb. 8 g
Fiber 3 g
Sodium 44 mg

APPLE FILLING

3 cups peeled, cored, and chopped
  apples

Enough water to cover

1 cup apple juice

⅓ to ½ teaspoon **powdered stevia
extract**

2 tablespoons lemon juice

1½ tablespoons cornstarch, or
  2 tablespoons arrowroot powder
  or quick tapioca

½ teaspoon cinnamon

¼ teaspoon nutmeg

• Place 1 cup of the apples in a medium-size saucepan. Cover with water and cook over medium heat.

• While the apples are cooking, process the other 2 cups of apples in a blender with the rest of the ingredients. If using quick tapioca let the blended ingredients sit for 15 minutes without heat.

• When the water is nearly gone in the pan add the blender mix. Bring to a boil then cook on low for 20 to 30 minutes, stirring occasionally, until the mixture is thick and the apple pieces are tender. If using quick tapioca bring to a full boil and cook until the tapioca turns clear and the apple pieces are tender.

• This sauce gets much thicker upon cooling. It is excellent served warm in crepes and turnovers or on pancakes.

NOTE: *If the apples are a softer variety, the cooking time may be reduced. The apple pieces should be tender not mushy. If the apple pieces are tender and there is still a lot of water left in the pan, discard some before adding the blender contents.*

VARIATION: *This recipe also works great with pears.*

Yield:
8 servings

Per serving:
Calories 46
Total Fat 0 g
Sat. Fat 0 g
Protein 0 g
Carb. 12 g
Fiber 1 g
Sodium 1 mg

STRAWBERRY FILLING

1 cup sliced, unsweetened, fresh or frozen strawberries

¾ cup unsweetened apple juice

¼ to ⅓ teaspoon **powdered stevia extract**

2 teaspoons honey, warmed (optional)

2 tablespoons rice or wheat flour

1 tablespoon cornstarch or arrowroot powder

1 tablespoon butter or margarine

2 ounces soft tofu

1 teaspoon lemon juice

• Place the berries and apple juice in a saucepan, and cook a few minutes until soft.

• Pour into a blender. Add the stevia extract and honey. Blend until smooth. Return to the pan. (Keep aside ½ cup of the berry sauce.) Heat on medium-low.

• Mix the flour and cornstarch or arrowroot powder into the remaining ½ cup of sauce. Stir the flour mixture into the hot berry sauce. Bring to a boil, stirring until the mixture is thick and smooth. If using cornstarch, reduce the heat and simmer on low for 5 minutes longer to be sure the starch is cooked. Remove from heat and beat in the butter or margarine. Chill.

• Cream the tofu and the lemon juice in a blender. Fold the creamed tofu into the cooled filling.

VARIATION: *Substitute any berry or fruit for the strawberries. Strain the seeds out of the berries by passing through a fine-mesh strainer after blending but before adding the starches.*

Yield: about 1⅓ cups (12 servings)

Per serving:
Calories 35
Total Fat 1 g
Sat. Fat 1 g
Protein 0 g
Carb. 6 g
Fiber <1 g
Sodium 11 mg

 JAM

1½ quarts fresh berries

1 cup unsweetened fruit juice concentrate

Pomona's Universal Pectin*

¾ teaspoon **powdered stevia extract**

• Follow the directions provided in the package of Pomona's Universal Pectin. Pomona's pectin can be used with sugar, honey, fruit juice, artificial sweetener, or stevia extract. Use the "All Fruit Recipes."

• Wash, rinse, and sterilize 4 (8-ounce) canning jars. Clean the berries, remove the hulls, and mash. To get 3 cups mashed berries, use 1½ quarts of fresh berries. Place in a saucepan.

• Add 4 teaspoons calcium water to the berries, and stir well. See the package directions for making calcium water.

• In another small saucepan, bring the juice concentrate to a boil. Place in a blender. Add 2 teaspoons of pectin powder and blend 1 to 2 minutes until the powder is dissolved.

• Bring the fruit to a boil in the saucepan. Add the dissolved pectin/juice concentrate. Stir vigorously for 1 minute. Stir in the stevia extract. Return to a boil and remove from the heat.

• Fill jars to ½-inch from the top. Screw on 2-piece lids. Boil for 5 minutes. Remove from the water and let the jars cool. Lids should pop to be sealed.

To purchase Pomona's see page 206.

Yield:
4 (8-ounce)
canning jars

Per
tablespoon:
Calories 9
Total Fat 0 g
Sat. Fat 0 g
Protein 0 g
Carb. 2 g
Fiber .4 g
Sodium 1 mg

# LEMON ICING

½ cup non-instant dry milk powder

¼ to ⅓ teaspoon **powdered stevia extract**

2 tablespoons butter or margarine, softened

2 tablespoons lemon juice

Finely grated rind of ½ lemon

1 tablespoon honey, or 2 tablespoons powdered sugar

2 to 4 tablespoons hot water

• Mix the milk powder and stevia extract together in a small bowl. Mix in the softened butter as best you can. Add the lemon juice, lemon rind, honey or powdered sugar, and water.

• Start with the lesser amount of water for a thick icing. For an icing that will run down the sides of a bundt cake or for a thin icing on sweet rolls, use the larger amount of water. Beat until smooth and fluffy.

• This is enough for a bundt cake or single-layer cake. Double the recipe for a double-layer cake.

NOTES: *If using powdered sugar, pass the milk powder, powdered sugar, and stevia extract through a fine-mesh strainer before adding the other ingredients.*

This icing gets very thick in the refrigerator. Try putting it in the refrigerator for 20 minutes, then adding 1 or 2 tablespoons more water before spreading it on the cake.

For a nondairy substitute, try to find a soymilk powder. (See Mail Order Sources for Ingredients, page 205.)

Yield:
about ⅔ cups
(10 servings)

Per serving:
(1 tablespoon)
Calories 60
Total Fat 4 g
Sat. Fat 3 g
Protein 2 g
Carb. 4 g
Fiber 0 g
Sodium 49 mg

CREAM CHEESE FROSTING

8 ounces soft cream cheese

2 tablespoons soymilk or milk

1½ tablespoons lemon juice

Finely grated rind of ½ lemon

⅓ to ½ teaspoon **powdered stevia extract** (to taste)

1 tablespoon honey

Yield:
about 1 cup
(10 servings)

Per serving:
Calories 84
Total Fat 8 g
Sat. Fat 5 g
Protein 2 g
Carb. 3 g
Fiber 0 g
Sodium 69 mg

• Soften the cream cheese with the milk in a bowl. Beat in the lemon juice, lemon rind, stevia extract, and honey. Whip until thoroughly blended and creamy.

FOR CHOCOLATE CREAM CHEESE FROSTING USE:

1 square of baker's chocolate

2 tablespoons honey

½ teaspoon **powdered stevia extract**

2 tablespoons soymilk or milk

1 teaspoon vanilla extract

8 ounces soft cream cheese

• Melt the chocolate in a heavy-bottomed pan on low. Mix in the honey and stevia extract. Mix the chocolate, milk, and vanilla into the cream cheese, and mix until well blended and creamy.

COCONUT FROSTING

1 cup unsweetened coconut

2 tablespoons butter or margarine, softened

¼ cup warm soymilk or milk

½ teaspoon vanilla extract

1 tablespoon honey, or 4 tablespoons powdered sugar

¼ teaspoon **powdered stevia extract**

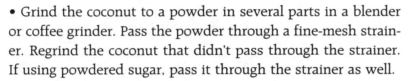

Yield:
about 1½
cups (12
servings)

Per serving:
Calories 151
Total Fat 14 g
Sat. Fat 12 g
Protein 1 g
Carb. 6 g
Fiber 3 g
Sodium 30 mg

• Grind the coconut to a powder in several parts in a blender or coffee grinder. Pass the powder through a fine-mesh strainer. Regrind the coconut that didn't pass through the strainer. If using powdered sugar, pass it through the strainer as well.

• Mix the butter or margarine into the coconut powder in a small bowl. Add the rest of the ingredients, and beat until well blended and creamy.

SERVING SUGGESTION: *Use as a filler between layers of a cake or spread on the top.*

🌿 "Whipped Cream"

½ cup raw cashews

½ cup soymilk

⅓ to ½ teaspoon **powdered stevia extract** (to taste)

½ teaspoon vanilla extract

2 teaspoons honey or maple syrup (optional)

Pinch of salt

½ cup oil

• Grind the cashews in a blender with the soymilk until creamy, using the pulse button. Periodically clean off the sides of the blender. Add the stevia extract, vanilla, honey or maple syrup, and salt. Blend until creamy.

• Slowly add the oil in a fine, steady stream through the center hole of the blender cover. Adding a few drops of water at this point may help thicken the cream. You may also have to use a little more oil.

NOTE: *A whipped cream can be made using ½ cup cashew nuts and ½ cup water plus the oil or simply by using ½ cup soymilk plus the oil. I have found that a thicker cream can be made by combining the cashew nuts with the soymilk. At times, however, the cream may not get thick enough. It seems to be influenced by the weather.*

Yield:
8 servings
(1 cup)

Per serving:
(2 tablespoons)
Calories 183
Total Fat 19 g
Sat. Fat 2 g
Protein 2 g
Carb. 4 g
Fiber .5 g
Sodium 17 mg

TOFU "WHIPPED CREAM"

1 (12.3-ounce) box silken tofu

3 tablespoons oil

⅓ to ½ teaspoon **powdered stevia extract** (to taste)

1½ tablespoons maple syrup or honey (optional)

¾ teaspoon vanilla extract

⅛ teaspoon salt

• Combine all the ingredients in a blender or food processor, and blend until smooth and creamy.

VARIATIONS: *Substitute citrus rind for the vanilla or add a few strawberries or other berries.*

Yield:
8 servings

Per serving:
Calories 69
Total Fat 6 g
Sat. Fat 1 g
Protein 2 g
Carb. 2 g
Fiber .3 g
Sodium 38 mg

CASHEW CREAM

½ cup raw cashews

1 cup water

1 tablespoon oil

⅓ to ½ teaspoon **powdered stevia extract** (to taste)

1 teaspoon maple syrup or honey (optional)

• Grind the cashews in part of the water. Add the rest of the water, the oil, stevia extract, and maple syrup or honey. Blend until smooth and creamy. Add a little more water if a thinner cream is desired.

Yield:
8 servings

Per serving:
Calories 70
Total Fat 6 g
Sat. Fat 1 g
Protein 1 g
Carb. 3 g
Fiber 0.3 g
Sodium 2 mg

# LEMON CREAM

A rich whipped topping for cakes, bars, puddings, or pie

½ cup raw cashews

½ cup soymilk

1½ tablespoons lemon juice

Finely grated rind of ½ lemon

⅓ to ½ teaspoon **powdered stevia extract** (to taste)

2 teaspoons honey (optional)

4 tablespoons melted butter or margarine

• Grind the cashews and soymilk together in a blender until smooth. Keep the sides of the blender scraped down. Blend in the lemon juice, rind, stevia extract, and honey.

• Place the mixture in a small mixing bowl. Melt the butter or margarine in a small pan or in the microwave. Gradually beat in the melted butter with a hand mixer. Beat on high for about 3 minutes until thick and creamy.

Yield:
8 servings

Per serving:
Calories 114
Total Fat 11 g
Sat. Fat 5 g
Protein 2 g
Carb. 4 g
Fiber .5 g
Sodium 65 mg

Frozen Desserts

❀ *Making Frozen Desserts* ❀

✳ **Electric Automatic Ice Cream Machine:** There are several brands of wonderful electric ice cream machines on the market today that don't require salt or ice. I bought a Cuisinart brand that works extremely well. The container is kept in the freezer overnight. The walls contain a substance that freezes. Simply plug in the machine and pour in the blended ingredients. (Chill the ingredients first if they were cooked on the stove.) The ice cream is ready in about 25 to 35 minutes.

TIP: After the ice cream is ready, remove the paddle, pack the ice cream down in the container, wrap a towel around it and place it in the refrigerator for about 20 minutes to 1½ hours to harden before serving. This will insure the best consistency and hardness. However, if you leave it too long the ice cream will get too hard and dry, so watch it. Pack any that is left over in a covered container, and place it in the freezer. Thaw about 15 minutes before serving again, if necessary.

✳ **Electric Churn Machine:** This machine requires alternating the outer container with layers of crushed ice and rock salt. Chill the mixture before pouring into the freezer can. When done, harden the ice cream for better texture by re-packing the container with ice and salt, removing the paddle, packing down the ice cream, and wrapping up the machine. Keep covered about 2 to 3 hours for best texture.

✳ **Hand Churned:** Follow directions for electric churned made with rock salt and ice. You do the work.

✳ **Refrigerator Method:** Prepare the mixture as above. Pour into a freezer tray or any flat pan. Freeze until mushy but not solid (between 1 and 2 hours). Place in a chilled bowl, and beat with chilled beaters until smooth. You will need to work quickly. Return the mixture to the tray and freeze hard. Remove from the freezer. Soften for about 10 to 15 minutes then beat in a blender or food processor until a smooth texture is achieved. Pack into covered containers and refreeze. Before serving, soften for about 15 minutes if necessary.

NOTE: If your ice cream does not get hard enough or has a coarse texture, try putting it in a container in the freezer and freezing it hard. Take it out and blend it in a blender or food processor until creamy. Serve immediately or refreeze in a covered container.

❀ HOLIDAY CRANBERRY SHERBET

**Growing up my mother served cranberry sherbet
every Thanksgiving and Christmas.**

1½ cups Creamy Cranberry Sauce (page 154), chilled

1 (12.3-ounce) box silken tofu, soft or firm

½ cup orange juice concentrate

½ teaspoon **powdered stevia extract**

1 teaspoon vanilla

1 tablespoon honey

• Prepare the Creamy Cranberry Sauce recipe on page 154. Chill well before using.

• Blend the tofu, orange juice, stevia extract, vanilla, and honey together in a blender until smooth. Blend in the cranberry sauce until very smooth and creamy.

• Pour the mixture into the container of an ice cream machine, and process according to directions, or follow the refrigerator method (page 169).

• Thaw about 15 minutes before serving, if necessary.

OPTION: *You may replace the tofu with 1 cup of half-and-half.*

Yield:
6 servings

Per serving:
Calories 173
Total Fat 3 g
Sat. Fat <1 g
Protein 5 g
Carb. 34 g
Fiber 2 g
Sodium 39 mg

# RASPBERRY SHERBET

This is absolutely delicious!

2 cups plain low-fat yogurt

¼ cup milk

½ cup unsweetened raspberry juice blend
concentrate, thawed

1 tablespoon orange juice concentrate

1 teaspoon vanilla extract

¾ teaspoon **powdered stevia extract**

1 banana (optional)

• Blend all the ingredients together in a blender until smooth.

• Pour into the container of an ice cream machine, and process according to directions, or use the refrigerator method (page 169).

NOTE: *It works very well to substitute a 12.3-ounce box of silken tofu for the yogurt. Use a total of 1 cup of milk.*

OPTION: *You may use any fruit juice blend concentrate of your choice.*

Yield:
4 servings

Per serving:
Calories 124
Total Fat 2 g
Sat. Fat 1 g
Protein 7 g
Carb. 19 g
Fiber 0.1 g
Sodium 98 mg

✿ Orange Sherbet

½ cup raw cashews

½ cup soymilk

2 tablespoons oil

1 tablespoon honey, warmed (optional)

1 cup orange juice from concentrate

½ cup papaya or mango juice or blend

1 teaspoon lemon juice

¾ teaspoon **powdered stevia extract**

Pinch of salt

1 tablespoon agar-agar

½ cup apple juice or water

• Grind the cashews in a blender with the soymilk until creamy. Add the oil, then the honey through the top of the blender in a fine stream. When creamy, add the orange juice, papaya or mango juice, lemon juice, stevia extract, and salt, and process.

• Place the agar in a small pan with the apple juice, and soak for 1 minute. Bring to a boil then simmer on low heat for about 3 to 5 minutes until dissolved. Blend into the other ingredients.

• Chill the ingredients before pouring into an ice cream machine. Follow the directions of your ice cream maker or use the refrigerator method (page 169).

Yield:
4 servings

Per serving:
Calories 367
Total Fat 31 g
Sat. Fat 4 g
Protein 4 g
Carb. 22 g
Fiber 1 g
Sodium 25 mg

see variations next page

NOTE: *Agar makes this sherbet very smooth. Be sure the agar has been thoroughly dissolved. For good flavor, make the orange juice strong.*

VARIATIONS: *Blend in a small banana or 2 tablespoons of coconut. If using coconut, grind it with the cashews. If more liquid is needed when grinding, use some of the orange juice.*

✿ QUICK BERRY ICE CREAM

6 medium-large, frozen bananas
2 cups frozen unsweetened berries
1 cup plain low-fat yogurt
½ teaspoon **powdered stevia extract**

• Slice the frozen bananas into a blender or food processor. Add the rest of ingredients and blend. If using a blender, use the pulse button. Between pulses stir the mixture. Process until smooth. Serve immediately.

Yield:
8 servings

Per serving:
Calories 111
Total Fat 1 g
Sat. Fat 0 g
Protein 3 g
Carb. 3 g
Fiber 4 g
Sodium 20 mg

✿ Frozen Fruit Yogurt

2 cups plain low-fat yogurt

1 cup fresh or frozen (thawed) unsweetened fruit

½ cup frozen unsweetened apple juice concentrate, thawed

2 tablespoons frozen orange juice concentrate

¾ teaspoon **powdered stevia extract**

1 teaspoon vanilla

• Blend all the ingredients together in a blender. If using raspberries or blackberries, press the blended ingredients through a fine-mesh strainer to remove seeds.

• Pour the contents into the container of the ice cream machine. Process according to directions or use the refrigerator method (page 169).

Yield:
4 servings

Per serving:
Calories 128
Total Fat 2 g
Sat. Fat 1 g
Protein 7 g
Carb. 21 g
Fiber 1 g
Sodium 92 mg

CHOCOLATE ICE CREAM

1½ squares baker's chocolate
3 tablespoons honey
1½ cups soymilk or milk
1 teaspoon vanilla
1 (12.3-ounce) box silken tofu
¾ teaspoon **powdered stevia extract**

• Melt the chocolate over low heat in a heavy-bottomed pan. Stir in the honey and several ounces of the soymilk or milk. Boil on low for 2 to 3 minutes. Add the rest of the milk and the vanilla.

• Blend the chocolate mixture, tofu, and stevia extract together in a blender until smooth. If still warm, chill the mixture in the refrigerator before pouring it into an ice cream maker.

• Process according to the directions of your ice cream machine.

OPTION: *You may replace the tofu and soymilk with 2 cups half-and-half and 1 cup whole milk.*

Yield:
4 servings

Per serving:
Calories 200
Total Fat 10 g
Sat. Fat 5 g
Protein 10 g
Carb. 23 g
Fiber 2 g
Sodium 76 mg

❀ Maple Nut Ice Cream

2 cups half-and-half

1 cup milk

2 tablespoons maple syrup (optional)

½ teaspoon maple flavoring

¾ teaspoon **powdered stevia extract**

½ cup chopped walnuts

• Blend all the ingredients together except the nuts. Pour into an ice cream machine, and process. Add the chopped walnuts about halfway into the freezing process. The nut pieces should be no bigger than a chocolate chip.

FOR VANILLA ICE CREAM USE:

2 cups half-and-half

1 cup milk

2 tablespoons honey (optional)

¾ teaspoon **powdered stevia extract**

1 tablespoon vanilla extract

• Blend all the ingredients together in a blender. Pour into the container of an ice cream machine, and process according to directions.

NOTE: *I found that the two recipes above did not work well using yogurt or tofu because the flavor was poor. However, you are welcome to try it for yourself.*

Yield:
6 servings

Per serving:
Calories 189
Total Fat 16 g
Sat. Fat 7 g
Protein 5 g
Carb. 7 g
Fiber .5 g
Sodium 54 mg

Yield:
6 servings

Per serving:
Calories 124
Total Fat 10 g
Sat. Fat 6 g
Protein 4 g
Carb. 5 g
Fiber 0 g
Sodium 53 mg

Stevia Products Comparison and Equivalency Chart

Product	Approximate Equivalency to Sugar
Stevia Tea Bags *dried green leaf in paper tea bags* 1 tea bag (will sweeten 2 cups of liquid)	2-3 teaspoons sugar
Stevia Leaf—Powdered *dried green leaf, finely powdered* 1 to 2 tablespoons green powdered leaf	1 cup sugar
Stevia Leaf—Cut and Sifted *dried green leaf cut from the stems and cleaned* 2 to 3 tablespoons crushed green leaf	1 cup sugar
Stevia Concentrate *green leaf simmered in water until thick and dark,* *then filtered* 1 teaspoon dark liquid concentrate	½ cup molasses
Stevia White Powdered Extract *sweet stevioside molecules extracted from the leaf* *and purified to a white powder* ⅓ to ½ teaspoon white powdered extract	1 cup sugar
Stevia White Powdered Extract with Filler *white powdered extract blended with either* *FOS or maltodextrin* 1½ to 2 tablespoons stevia extract/filler	1 cup sugar
Stevia Clear Liquid Extract *white powdered extract reconstituted with water* ½ teaspoon clear liquid extract	1 cup sugar

All the above are products you can buy from an herb company, health food store, or mail order source. A liquid herbal extract can be made at home (see page 15).

Substitutions

1 teaspoon baking powder	=	⅓ teaspoon baking soda + ½ teaspoon cream of tartar + ⅛ teaspoon salt
	or	½ teaspoon baking soda + ½ cup buttermilk or yogurt
	or	½ teaspoon baking soda + 1½ teaspoons lemon juice
1 cup buttermilk	=	1 cup yogurt
	or	1 cup soured milk
1 tablespoon cornstarch	=	1 tablespoon arrowroot powder
	or	1 tablespoon quick tapioca
	or	1 tablespoon potato flour
	or	2 tablespoons wheat or rice flour
1 egg (as a binder)	=	¼ cup nut butter
	or	2 ounces tofu
	or	½ ripe banana
	or	½ teaspoon guar gum
	or	¼ cup apple butter
	or	use packaged powdered egg replacer
1 tablespoon vegetarian gelatin	=	2 tablespoons agar flakes
1 ounce unsweetened baker's chocolate	=	3 tablespoons cocoa + 1 tablespoon oil

Measures

60 drops	=	1 teaspoon
1 tablespoon	=	3 teaspoons
2 tablespoons	=	1 ounce
4 tablespoons	=	¼ cup or 2 ounces
5⅓ tablespoons	=	⅓ cup or 2⅔ ounces
8 tablespoons	=	½ cup or 4 ounces
16 tablespoons	=	1 cup or 8 ounces
1 pint	=	2 cups or 16 ounces
1 quart	=	4 cups, 2 pints, or 32 ounces
1 gallon	=	16 cups or 4 quarts

Food Preparation Tips

BLANCHING ALMONDS: Boil 1 cup of water or enough to cover the nuts. Pour the boiling water over the nuts in a bowl. Let set 1 minute. Drain and slip off the skins with your thumb and index finger.

CAROB: The pod of the tamarind tree is naturally sweet. Its finely ground powder contains many minerals but no stimulants. Carob can be substituted in recipes calling for chocolate. It can be purchased raw or roasted. The raw is lighter in color and weight and more delicate in flavor. Roasted carob has a very intense dominating flavor so the amount called for in the recipes may have to be reduced, e.g. from ½ cup to ⅓ cup.

CAROB SYRUP: Some recipes are improved if you prepare a carob syrup first. Use the following directions.

In a small saucepan, mix 1 cup of carob powder with 1 cup of water. Cook over at a low boil for 5 to 8 min-utes stirring continually until smooth and creamy. If it is too thick, add a little more water.

CHOCOLATE AND COCOA: Cocoa is made from the hulled beans of an evergreen tree in the genus *Theobroma.* Part of the cocoa butter has been removed from the hulled bean to make cocoa while cocoa butter is added to the bean to make baker's chocolate. Cocoa has significantly less calories. **Three tablespoons of cocoa is equal to 1 square of baker's chocolate.**

I included chocolate recipes in the book because so many people love it. However, I was unable to completely offset the bitterness of cocoa or baker's chocolate with stevia alone, and I prefer using a little honey. On the next page I give the ratio that I found works well and gives an excellent flavor and texture:

At least 2 tablespoons of honey or equivalent with 1 square of baker's chocolate, or 3 tablespoons of cocoa plus ½ to ¾ teaspoon stevia extract.

Three tablespoons of honey would improve the flavor and texture even more. If you love chocolate and can eat a little sweetener, try the chocolate recipes in this book.

CRANBERRIES: The tartness of these berries can be relieved some by soaking the cranberries whole or chopped in stevia extract for several hours or overnight in the refrigerator.

EGGS: Yolks add richness, moistness, and tenderness to baked goods. The whites act as a leavening. Eggs also bind the ingredients together. Try to buy eggs from cage-free or free-running hens. I love the thought of hens running around being themselves and doing their thing.

FROZEN FRUIT: Frozen fruit, especially bananas, make blender drinks thick and creamy. To freeze bananas, peel first and place in an air tight container or freezer bag. I wrap them individually in wax paper then put them in a freezer bag. Bananas will turn brown after 10 to 14 days in the freezer. Keep other frozen fruit in your freezer for year-round versatility. Berries and other fruit are usually much cheaper frozen than fresh and sometimes they are better quality.

FROZEN FRUIT JUICE CONCENTRATES, FRUIT SAUCES, FRUIT PURÉES: Keep some of these around the house for variety in flavor. Add several tablespoons of juice concentrate to muffins or cakes for extra zing. Try plum sauce instead of applesauce for a different flavor. Unsweetened fruit purées (or fruit butters) are wonderful. A little can be added to whipped cream or frosting. It can be used by itself between cake layers. (See Product Directory, page 206.)

HIGH ALTITUDE BAKING: Adjustments to recipes may be required as altitude increases. Adjustments vary depending on whether baking cakes, cookies, etc. and how high the altitude is. Some of the changes include: under-beating the eggs, raising baking temperatures about 25°F, and reducing the baking powder. See a standard cookbook for more details.

MAKING BAKING POWDER: Single-acting: to replace 1 teaspoon of baking powder sift together:

$\frac{1}{2}$ teaspoon cream of tartar
$\frac{1}{3}$ teaspoon baking soda
$\frac{1}{8}$ teaspoon salt

MAKING OAT FLOUR: Spread oat flakes on a cookie sheet. Toast in 300°F oven for 15 to 20 minutes until golden brown. Grind in a blender to a fine flour.

MAKING SOUR MILK: Add 1 tablespoon of fresh lemon juice or vinegar to 1 cup soymilk or whole milk. Let stand for 10 minutes.

MEASURE ACCURATELY: All given measurements are level, unless otherwise noted. "Scant" denotes slightly less than the full amount. "Heaping" means a rounded mound above level. To "pack" an ingredient press down on the substance until all the air is out.

MILK: There are a number of milks commercially available other than dairy. In recipes calling for milk, use dairy, soy, or rice milk. Oat milk is also available. These can be purchased fresh or in aseptic cartons with a long shelf life. Also nut and seed milks can be made. (See the almond or cashew milk recipes on page 34.) Soymilk works very well in everything. I could not get rice milk to thicken with cornstarch or arrowroot powder when making pudding.

OVEN PLACEMENT: Place oven racks where you want them while the oven is cold. The usual position is on a rack slightly above center. Try placing pans on a rack just below center for cakes and quick breads that are browning too fast. Place a single pan in the middle of the oven. Have 2 inches between 2 pans on the same shelf and 2 inches from all four walls of the oven. If using 2 shelves, stagger the pans.

OVER-MIXING of quick breads and muffins results in a coarse texture filled with holes and tunnels.

PAN SIZE: Cake batter should fill the pan no less than half and no more than $\frac{2}{3}$ full. If the pan is too large, the cake will not rise properly.

If the pan is too small, the texture will be coarse and the batter may overflow or sink upon cooling. Loaf pans may be filled to ¾ full. Fill muffin pans to ¾ or full.

PIE CRUSTS: If you have trouble rolling out crusts, use two sheets of waxed paper or use pastry cloth and a rolling pin cover. All the ingredients need to be cold. If the room is very hot, you must work quickly. Try chilling the pie dough for 15 to 20 minutes and then let it warm up for about 5 minutes before rolling it out. To prevent a soggy bottom crust, brush with egg white or melted butter or partially bake the crust. Pies with a filling like pumpkin can be partially baked for 15 minutes at 350°F. Remove from the oven, cool, pour in the filling, and continue baking. For a golden brown crust, brush the top crusts with an egg wash made of 1 egg and ¼ cup milk. Refer to the book *Fruit Sweet and Sugar Free* by Janice Feuer for expert pie crust making advice.

PREHEATING AN OVEN: It can take up to 20 minutes to get an oven up to the right temperature. Even newer ovens that heat up in 5 minutes may not have an even temperature for 15 to 20 minutes.

PREPARATION: It is generally advised that all ingredients be brought to room temperature before mixing. I start warming everything up, including the room, by turning on the oven and taking everything out of the refrigerator before I begin. The only exception is in making pie crust where all the ingredients must be cold. Also, avoid over-warming eggs and butter in hot weather.

RANCIDITY: Buy only fresh, raw nuts and seeds. As with oils (except olive oil), store in the refrigerator. When fats spoil, they are said to be rancid. Oxygen, in the presence of heat and light, reacts with the unsaturated double bonds in the fat. This reaction produces peroxides, free radicals that cause physiological damage. Oils, nuts, and whole grains contain the natural antioxidants vitamins E and C. These are eventually used up in preventing fat decomposition. Rancid oils have a bitter taste.

High frying temperatures of 400°F and above begin destroying unsaturated fatty acids. Smoking is a sign of the oil going bad.

REFRIGERATOR COOKIES: The trick is preventing the incorporation of too much flour when rolling out the dough. Using a rolling pin cover and pastry cloth may help.

RICE FLOUR AND CORN MEAL: To eliminate grittiness, mix the flour or meal with the liquid in a recipe, and heat to boiling while stirring.

STORING BAKED GOODS: For longer-lasting freshness, store baked goods made with whole foods in the refrigerator or freezer if not eaten the same day. To freeze, cut cakes and bars into individual servings first. Bring back the freshness of a refrigerated or frozen baked item by placing an individual serving in a microwave oven for about 15 to 25 seconds (about 25 to 35 seconds if frozen). It's amazing how light and tender cakes and muffins become after a short time in the microwave. The sweetness and flavor of some stevia-sweetened foods improves after they have cooled in the refrigerator or have been frozen for a day or two. Cookies will be fine on the counter for 2 days loosely covered or in a cookie jar. (They may stay crispier than if they were stored in a refrigerator). Cakes, unless they have an icing or filling that needs refrigeration, can also be kept on the counter for a day or two in a covered container or wrap, such as foil, that allows some air flow. In hot weather though, refrigerate leftovers before going to bed.

STORING SPICES AND HERBS: Buy dried spices and herbs as fresh as possible. Health food stores and herb shops are good places to buy for better prices and fresher spices. Store spices and herbs in covered glass containers in a dry closed cupboard. Spices stay fresh for about 1 year.

SWEETENERS: There are two forms of sweeteners: granular and liquid. If you are able to eat some sweetener, you can use any from the following list. If the recipe calls for a granular sweetener, choose from the following granular list. If the recipe calls for liquid sweetener, choose from the following liquid list. Some people can tolerate one type of sweetener better than another. I have found that the addition of even a tiny amount of sweetener improves flavor and makes the food more satisfying, especially when no fruit is called for. In this book, sweetener is used more like a condiment. **Don't use any additional sweeteners if you can't tolerate them.**

Granular Sweeteners
    date sugar
    raw sugar
    xylitol – birch sugar
    brown sugar
Liquid Sweeteners
    maple syrup
    rice syrup/barley malt
    honey
    molasses

TESTING BAKING POWDER: Place 1 teaspoon of powder in ⅓ cup hot water. Use if it bubbles effervescently.

THICKENERS: There are two basic types of thickening agents, starches and gelatins.

Starches

Cornstarch: A refined powder processed from the endosperm of the corn kernel. Used to thicken puddings and sauces. Care is necessary in preventing both the undercooking and overcooking of the starch.

Arrowroot powder: The beaten pulp of the tuberous root stocks of the tropical American maranta plant. Thickens sauces, puddings, and glazes after several minutes of cooking on low heat. It thickens quickly with little trouble, but the texture is not as smooth and creamy as with cornstarch.

Tapioca: Milled from the dried starch of the cassava root. Must be brought to the boiling point then removed from the heat. Tapioca thickens as it cools. Used for sauces, puddings, and glazes. Often used to thicken fruit pies.

This starch needs to set in the cold liquid before cooking. In milk, let it set for 5 minutes. In acid fruits like berries, let it set for 15 minutes. Cook until the liquid comes to a full boil and until the white pellets have turned clear.

Kudzu (or kuzu) root: A powder made from a vine that originally was grown in the Far East, but now is a widespread, invasive plant found throughout the southeastern U.S. It is dissolved in a small amount of liquid, then added to other simmering liquids. Kudzu thickens without boiling. Used for sauces, puddings, and glazes.

Potato starch: Made from cooked potatoes that have been dried and ground. Generally used in soups and gravies.

Wheat or rice flour: May be used to thicken sauces and puddings. You need to use twice as much as the other thickeners listed here. You may use them in combination with other thickeners.

Gelatins

Agar–agar: Boiled and dried seaweed, also known as kanten. Use 1 tablespoon to 1 cup of liquid. Place the agar in the liquid, and bring to a boil. Reduce the heat and simmer about 5 minutes until the agar is dissolved. Thickens to a clear gel upon cooling.

Vegetarian gelatin: contains carrageenan, locust bean gum, and maltodextrin. Use the same amount of vegetarian gelatin to replace regular gelatin in any recipe.

TOFU: Tofu can be purchased fresh or in aseptic packages that have a long shelf life. Don't use old, sour-smelling tofu for blender drinks, puddings, or cheesecakes. Tofu in aseptic cartons always tastes fresh and works better for uncooked foods. These cartons can be kept on your shelf for months. Tofu is measured by weight in the recipes in this book. To measure boxed tofu, cut the carton open with a scissors on three sides. They weigh about 12 ounces. You can easily cut off the portion needed: 6 ounces (half a carton), 4 ounces (a third of a carton), etc. For blender drinks, puddings, and cakes use a soft tofu. For cheesecakes and pie fillings use a firm tofu.

Fresh tofu can be stored in the refrigerator for about 1 week if kept covered with water in a tightly covered container. Change the water every day or so for greater freshness. Sour-smelling tofu may still be used for cooking. Either shave off the outer portions or boil the cake in water for 20 minutes. Leftover vacuum-packed tofu doesn't keep as long in the refrigerator as fresh tofu. See storage directions on the outside of the carton.

VARIABLES: There are a number of variables in baking including the size of the eggs, moisture content of foods, bakeware, oven proficiency, measuring and mixing techniques, temperature of ingredients, and weather. For instance, at times, I can't get cashew or soy whipped cream to bind which may be related to certain weather conditions. It's very important to get to know your oven and your baking pans. If you are consistently having trouble, adjustments must be made.

Ingredients Glossary

AGAR-AGAR Flakes or bars derived from sea algae. Used as a gelling agent in place of animal gelatin. It supplies bulk and lubrication in the intestinal tract and increases peristaltic action, thus relieving constipation.

ALMONDS The fruit of a small tree related to the peach. High in protein, B vitamins, and the minerals calcium, phosphorus, and iron. This healthful nut can be made into almond butter, almond milk, or ground into a meal.

APPLE BUTTER The pulp of apples, cooked, strained, and cooked further until thick and creamy. Several unsweetened brands are available.

ARROWROOT POWDER A starch from the tuberous roots of a tropical American plant used as a thickening agent in sauces and puddings. It is high in minerals and easily digested. Can be used as substitute for cornstarch. Basic proportions for a sauce are **1½ tablespoons of arrowroot to 1 cup of liquid.**

BANANA CHIPS Banana slices that have been dried to a crispy texture. Sweetened and unsweetened varieties are available. They can be coarsely ground in a blender and added to cookie batter to add a crispy texture.

BRAN The outer layers of grain. Bran absorbs moisture, providing bulk in the intestinal tract. Oat and wheat bran are most often used. Bran absorbs liquid in baked goods as well, which may lead to a dry or crumbly product if too much is added.

BROWN RICE Whole, unpolished rice. Not separated from its bran and germ as white rice is.

BUTTERMILK   Originally this was the residue from the butter churn. Today it is generally made from pasteurized skim milk with a culture added to produce a heavier consistency and to develop flavor.

COCONUT   The fruit of the coconut palm contains a thick, edible meat and a milk. Unsweetened shredded coconut can be purchased in health food stores.

CAROB POWDER   Finely ground pod of the tamarind, also called St. John's Bread. An excellent bowel conditioner, it is also high in minerals, very alkaline, and rich in natural sugars. Used as an alternative to chocolate. Can be purchased raw or roasted. The raw is lighter and more delicate in flavor. (See page 180 for more information about carob.)

CASHEWS   The cashew nut is the seed of the cashew apple, which grows on the outside of the fruit. A tropical American tree of the sumac family, cashews are a good source of vitamins D and B_1 (thiamine), iron, protein, and unsaturated fats. This soft, versatile nut can be blended to a smooth, white liquid that replaces dairy products such as milk, cream, and whipped cream. Cashews can also be processed into an excellent nut butter.

CORNSTARCH   A fine powder derived from the endosperm of the corn kernel. Used as a thickening agent; it will taste starchy if under-cooked. Cornstarch makes clear, smooth-textured sauces and puddings. It causes digestive problems and allergic reactions in some people.

CRANBERRIES   The tart berries of a shrub related to blueberries (*Vaccinium*), native to the bog habitat of eastern North America but now grown commercially in ponds.

DATE SUGAR   Dehydrated and pulverized dates. I prefer a brown, somewhat coarse date sugar. I've been seeing a very light-colored and powdery form on the market lately that I don't care for.

EGGS   Use eggs from free-running or cage-free chickens if possible. Chickens suffer tremendously on large commercial farms. Eggs leaven baked goods and bind ingredients together.

EGG REPLACER A powdered product is available consisting of potato starch, tapioca flour, leavening, and vegetable gums. Also, tofu, nut butters, apple butter, and banana act as binders in a recipe.

FLOUR Wheat flour's superb rising ability is due to its high gluten content. This quality has made wheat flour the norm for bakers. A number of other flours are available that may be used, in whole or in part, to add flavor and variety to baked goods. Some flours may produce a heavier dough and more leavening may be required. I recommend using whole grain flours as much as possible. Enriched white flours only replace several of the 20 or more nutrients removed with the germ in the refining process. Whole grain flours should be refrigerated or frozen to maintain freshness.

Amaranth The seed of an ancient plant used by the Aztecs. A nutritionally superior food that can be ground into a flour.

Barley A smooth, mild-flavored grain and a very good substitute for wheat flour. Contains a small amount of gluten.

Corn Ground whole kernel corn, finer than cornmeal.

Oat You may buy oat flour or grind it from toasted oat flakes (see page 182). Use in small amounts as a dry product may result.

Quinoa The seed of an ancient Andean plant related to spinach. A nutritional superfood, delicately flavored, that may be used whole like millet or ground into a flour.

Rice Rice finely ground to make rice flour. It contains no gluten but has a gritty quality.

Soy   Soy is high in protein. Never eat uncooked because it contains an enzyme that blocks digestion. You can purchase toasted soy flour. Soy flour is also 20% fat. Its strong flavor restricts use to no more than 25% of the total flour in a recipe. Soy flour makes a tender, moist, and nicely browned product.

Spelt   A variety of hard wheat often tolerated by those allergic to regular wheat flours.

Wheat   Available in hard and soft varieties and further classified as spring or winter wheat, referring to the season in which it is planted.

Hard wheat varieties have a high gluten content and are the best for baking bread. Stone-ground whole wheat is the coarsest grade but retains the most nutrients.

Soft wheat varieties are ground into pastry flour. They are low in gluten and do not rise as well. However, they are finer and more suitable for baking. Whole wheat pastry flour is recommended.

Unbleached white flour is refined and enriched but has not been put through a bleaching process. It can be used when a lighter, finer texture is desired.

FOS (fructooligosaccharide)   A carbohydrate found naturally in fruits, vegetables, and grain. It cannot be digested or absorbed by humans but supports the growth of beneficial bacteria in the colon.

FRUITSOURCE A wonderful granular or liquid sweetener derived from grapes and rice. Currently available only in bulk directly from the company. See Product Directory, page 206, for phone number listing.

GUAR GUM   The ground seed of an East Indian legume called *Cyanopsis psoralioides*. It is used as a thickener for salad dressings, ice creams, puddings, gravies, and sauces. Helps egg-free quick breads rise and hold together.

HONEY   Produced by bees from the nectar of flowers. Sweeter than sugar, use moderately.

KUDZU   A leguminous vine native to Japan growing up to 30 feet tall. It has become a destructive, invasive plant in the southern United States. A white starch used as a thickener for puddings and sauces is obtained from the roots. It is called kuzu in Japan.

LEAVENINGS   Quick rising in baked goods can be accomplished by using baking soda or baking powder. Baking soda (sodium bicarbonate) interacts with acidic ingredients such as buttermilk, yogurt, fruit juices, vinegar, molasses, and honey. Carbon dioxide bubbles are released that are locked into place by heat.

Baking powders contain both the alkaline and the acidic components; usually sodium bicarbonate with either tartaric acid, calcium acid phosphate, or sodium aluminum sulfate. These compounds interact to form carbon dioxide. Tartaric acid powders are single-acting with the action taking place in the cold batter. See page 182 for making your own baking powder.

Double-acting baking powders start work in the cold dough and have additional rising action in the heat of the oven. Phosphate powders are double-acting, but most of their action takes place in the cold batter. Most of the action of aluminum powders takes place in a hot oven. They are more effective, but for health reasons, aluminum-free baking powders are recommended.

In recipes containing acid ingredients, both baking powder and baking soda are often used. A small amount of soda is needed to neutralize the acid and less baking powder is required.

Keep leavenings to a minimum; generally no more than 1 teaspoon per cup of flour.

LECITHIN   Phosphatides extracted primarily from soybeans. Lecithin emulsifies cholesterol in the blood, breaks up fats into small particles, and regulates the deposit of fat in the liver. It may be added to baked goods and other foods.

MALTODEXTRIN A carbohydrate made from cornstarch. The starch is cooked and treated with acid or enzymes to break down the complex molecules into dextrose polymers that are easy to digest. It is used as a filler in other foods to add bulk and to keep dry foods free flowing. Maltodextrin contains 4 calories/gram and has a glycemic index metabolically equivalent to glucose though is not sweet tasting.

MAPLE SYRUP The boiled down, concentrated sap of the maple tree. Use genuine maple syrup.

MAPLE FLAVORING A concentrated natural flavoring in a glycerin base. I do not recommend imitation flavorings.

MEAL Coarsely ground grains, nuts, and seeds. Meal is easier to digest than whole nuts.

MARGARINE Some of the recipes call for butter or margarine. Most margarines are considered harmful to your health due to the presence of trans-fatty acids. However there are several margarines now available that are non-hydrogenated and contain no trans-fatty acids. Look for these in your local natural foods store, or you may sometimes find them in the larger supermarkets.

Another brand, Caneleo, has 16% trans-fatty acids. I can tolerate this margarine better over others of its type. See the Product Directory, page 206, for sources of this and other natural margarines.

MOLASSES Blackstrap molasses is a byproduct of the early stages of white sugar refinement. It is rich in minerals, especially iron and calcium. Blackstrap molasses is more a flavoring agent than a sweetener. Barbados molasses is also made from sugar cane but it is not a byproduct. The juice of the sugar cane is extracted, filtered, and boiled down to a syrup. The mineral content is low compared to blackstrap. It is the starting substance for making rum. Sorghum molasses is made in a similar way to Barbados molasses but is made from another grass species, sorghum, instead of sugar cane.

OIL   Cold-pressed oils retain their nutrients. Safflower and canola oil are mild-flavored, all-purpose oils containing over 90% polyunsaturated fats. Corn oil is strong-flavored and heavy. Sunflower oil has a slightly sweet and buttery taste and contains about 60% polyunsaturated fats. Store oils (except olive oil) in the refrigerator to retain freshness.

PEANUT BUTTER   The seeds of a legume that ripen in a pod underground. Use nonhydrogenated natural peanut butter for baking.

POPPYSEEDS   This seed comes from a different species than the opium poppy. Seeds may be roasted, steamed, or crushed to release more flavor.

RICE MILK   A naturally sweet, pleasant-tasting, and low-fat extract of brown rice. In my experience, rice milk will not thicken with cornstarch or arrowroot powder.

SEA SALT   Sea water that has been vacuum dried at low temperatures. Contains all the sea water minerals.

SESAME SEEDS   The seed of an herb. Very high in magnesium, calcium, lecithin, and amino acids. Yields a flavorful oil high in unsaturated fats. Makes a nutritious milk suitable for children.

SESAME TAHINI   A butter made from ground white sesame seeds. It is 45% protein and 55% unsaturated oils. It is a nutritious and versatile substitute for a number of dairy products.

SOYMILK   A beverage made from soybeans that can be substituted in equal parts for dairy milk. The fat content varies, so read the label. Most brands are sweetened, although unsweetened milk is usually available.

For making sour milk, unsweetened soymilk seems to curdle better than sweetened varieties. Soymilk thickens well with cornstarch, arrowroot powder, and tapioca. It can be purchased in convenient, aseptic packages that have a long shelf life.

SUNFLOWER SEEDS   A nutritious and economical substitute for nuts, sunflowers are packed with magnesium, calcium, phosphorus, and unsaturated fats. They can be blended with nuts to make milk.

TAPIOCA   A starch from the root of the tropical cassava plant used as a thickener in making sauces and puddings.

TOFU   A white curd made from soybeans and a coagulant in a process similar to cheese making. An inexpensive and versatile source of protein. It is measured by weight in the recipes in this book.

VANILLA   An extract of the seed pod of a tropical American climbing orchid.

YOGURT   Cow's milk cultured with bacteria that is beneficial to the intestinal tract. Also available made from goat's milk and soymilk.

ZEST   The colored, outer portion of oranges, tangerines, lemons, and limes. Zest contains high concentrations of flavorful oils. Avoid grating the bitter white layer underneath. Wash and dry the fruit before grating.

Shopping List

Some of the stevia products can be purchased in a health food store; others may have to be ordered by mail from an herb company. See page 204 for a list of herb companies. You may get a better price if you order all your stevia products from an herb company.

The **starred items** will probably have to be purchased in a health food store. Nuts, seeds, dried fruit, and sometimes nut butters can be found in a good fruit stand or specialty store like Trader Joes, or in a health food store. Many of these ingredients can be purchased in a regular grocery store. It's a good idea to buy spices and poppyseeds in a health food store; they are much cheaper and fresher.

STEVIA PRODUCTS
*Powdered or clear liquid extract
*Stevia leaf—powdered or
cut and dried
Stevia concentrate
(order from Wisdom Herbs)
Stevia tea bags
(order from Wisdom Herbs)

RAW NUTS AND SEEDS
(not roasted or salted)

almonds	cashews
walnuts	pecans
sunflower seeds	sesame seeds

NUT BUTTERS
(roasted or raw O.K.)
*almond butter
*cashew butter
*sesame tahini
peanut butter (natural)

FLAVORINGS—(not imitation)
vanilla extract
almond extract
*maple flavoring (This may have to be ordered, but it's worth it. See Product Directory, page 206)

FLOUR/GRAINS

*whole wheat pastry flour
 unbleached white flour
*soy flour
*rice flour
*barley—for variety
whole wheat bread flour (hard wheat) if making yeast dough
rolled oats (regular or quick)
bran (wheat or oat)
short grain brown or white rice

THICKENERS

*arrowroot powder or kudzu
quick tapioca
cornstarch
*agar-agar
*vegetarian gelatin

SPICES

cinnamon   nutmeg
cloves   allspice
cardamom   salt
ginger, dried and fresh

SWEETENERS

honey or malt syrup
maple syrup
blackstrap molasses
*date sugar

DAIRY PRODUCTS or ALTERNATES

milk—dairy, soy, or other
yogurt—non-fat and/or low-fat, dairy or soy
low-fat cottage cheese
*tofu—soft, medium, or firm (aseptically packed recommended)
whipping cream (heavy cream)
buttermilk
half-and-half
cream cheese
butter or margarine
*non-instant dry milk powder, dairy or soy (may be difficult to find)

DRIED FRUIT

raisins   figs
dates   apricots
banana chips

FRUIT JUICES (unsweetened, bottled or frozen)

apple or a blend
pineapple or a blend
mango or papaya or a blend

*Starred items may have to be purchased in a health food store.

FROZEN FRUIT JUICE CONCENTRATES (unsweetened)

apple
*cran-apple
*apple raspberry
orange

FRUITS—*fresh (f), fresh or frozen (ff)*

apples—f
lemons—f
oranges—f
bananas—f
pears—ff
plums—ff
cranberries—ff
peaches—ff
blueberries—ff
strawberries—ff
raspberries—ff
blackberries—ff

MISCELLANEOUS FRUIT

(unsweetened)
applesauce
apple butter
jam
*coconut

VEGETABLES

carrots   zucchini
squash   pumpkin
yams or sweet potatoes

LEAVENINGS

baking soda
*baking powder (non-aluminum)
yeast (for making breakfast rolls)

MISCELLANEOUS

bottles of sparkling water
granola
eggs, free-range or cage-free
cold-pressed safflower or canola oil
poppyseeds
cocoa
*carob—raw or roasted
chocolate or carob chips
*ginger snaps or graham crackers—
MI-DEL brand or other
*Pomona's Universal Pectin
(for making jam)

*Starred items may have to be
purchased in a health food store.*

Useful Equipment

Basting Brush—for applying butter and glazes to pie or bread crust.

Blender (Multi-speed)—indispensable. I've had the same 10-speed Osterizer blender for nearly 20 years.

Cheese Cloth—for separating liquid from pulp.

Colander—for washing and draining fruits and vegetables.

Cookie Cutters

Cooling Racks—to cool baked goods whether in the pan or out. Circulates air for faster cooling.

Cutting Boards—Have a separate board for cutting fruit and working with bread or cookie batter. This will keep them from absorbing onion and garlic odors. If made from wood, the boards must be scoured periodically with lemon, baking soda, or bleach.

Food Processor—great for chopping, grinding, and blending.

Graters—4-sided grater, wooden ginger grater.

Grater Brush—a small wire brush that makes a frustrating job easy.

Grinders—Nut grinder, nutmeg grinder if you like to use fresh whole nutmeg.

Hand Blender or Mini Food Processor—The high-speed Braun is useful for blender drinks, sauces, and dressings—convenient and less clean-up time. A mini food processor will cream tofu and grind nuts.

Juicer—Squeeze citrus by using a hand or electric juicer.

Measuring Cups and Spoons—graduated glass cups in 1 and 2 cup sizes, and larger if desired. One stainless steel or plastic nesting cup set. Two metal or plastic, nesting measuring spoon sets.

Mixing Bowls—Several large, medium, and small deep bowls. Either glass, ceramic, or stainless steel. Lighter weight bowls are more practical.

Mixer—Small, electric hand mixers are helpful in making cakes, whipping eggs, and making frosting.

Oven Thermometer—Oven temperatures may differ from the gauge especially in older stoves. Oven thermometers are not considered accurate either. Get a good thermometer to check the temperature while baking or just get to know your oven.

Pastry Blender—For cutting fat into flour.

Pastry Cloth and Cover for a **Rolling Pin**—Helpful in reducing the introduction of too much flour when rolling out refrigerator cookies and pie crusts.

Pot Holders—Gloves or pads. Use nice, thick ones.

Rolling Pin—For rolling out pie crusts and cookie dough.

Saucepans—Having several Pyrex glass saucepans is recommended. They are wonderful for making puddings and sauces, stewing fruit, and melting chocolate. You never have to worry if metal is getting into the food, and they clean up easily.

Sifter—For thoroughly combining dry ingredients. Use a triple sifter. Never wash a sifter.

Spatulas—Rubber spatulas for cleaning out the blender and the bowl. A straight-edge wooden spatula works well for stirring puddings.

Strainers—A fine-mesh tea strainer for straining the pulp and seeds from citrus fruit. A hand-held 5-inch fine-mesh strainer.

Timer—Never forget again!

Whisks—For whipping eggs and combining liquid ingredients.

Wooden Spoons—Solid and slotted.

BAKEWARE

The choice of baking pans makes a difference in the baking temperature, baking times, and the quality of the finished product.

Dark bakeware and glass absorb and hold heat. Therefore, food cooked in such pans needs to bake at a 10° to 25°F lower temperature than food cooked in shiny metal pans which deflect heat. If the food is cooking too fast, it will brown quickly on the outside but not get done on the inside. When using dark bakeware, watch the item closely near the end of the baking time. Cover with foil if the surface is getting too brown.

Heavier bakeware is better because it absorbs, retains, and distributes heat evenly. Light-weight cake pans and cookie sheets have dead or hot spots. You may double-pan a thin cake pan.

There is evidence that aluminum from non-anodized aluminum cookware dissolves into food and causes a whole range of health problems. Non-anodized aluminum cookware is banned in some countries. But in the U.S., it is widely used in homes, restaurants, and in the processed food industry. Choose an alternate material when possible. See the list of recommended bakeware below.

Recommended Bakeware

2 (8-inch) round cake pans

1 or 2 (9-inch) round cake pans

1 (10 to 12 cup) Tube or Bundt pan

1 (8 or 9-inch) Springform pan

2 (8-inch) square baking pans
   (1 shallow sided, 1 deep)

1 (6 x 10-inch) baking pan

1 (11 x 7-inch) baking pan

1 (9 x 13-inch) glass baking pan

1 or 2 medium-size loaf pans

3 (6 count) muffin pans

1 large cookie sheet

2 (9-inch) pie pans

1 (9½-inch) glass deep-dish pie pan

1 medium-size covered casserole
   dish

Resources

STEVIA BOOKS

The Stevia Story by Linda Bonvie, Bill Bonvie, and Donna Gates
  The history, politics and uses of stevia, some recipes

Stevia: Nature's Sweet Secret by David Richard
  History, cultivation, pharmacology, and research, some recipes

The Miracle of Stevia by James May
  Research, history, politics, health benefits, some recipes

COOKBOOKS

Below is a list of cookbooks that gave me inspiration or instruction in whole foods cooking and/or low sugar baking. I thank all these cooks and bakers for their hard work and contribution to wholesome cooking.

The American Vegetarian Cookbook from the Fit for Life Kitchen by Marilyn Diamond. *A complete cookbook including desserts for healthy living.*

The Book of Whole Meals by Annemarie Colbin, Ballantine Books, New York, 1979. *Simple wholesome meals, including desserts, that follow the seasons.*

Desserts to Lower Your Fat Thermostat by Barbara W. Higa, Vitality House International, Inc., Provo, Utah, 1988. *Cooks and bakes with frozen fruit juice concentrates.*

Fruit Sweet and Sugar Free by Janice Feuer, Healing Arts Press, 1993. *Professional baker and pastry chef. Cooks and bakes with a concentrated fruit sweetener and whole grains. Very instructional.*

Naturally Delicious Desserts and Snacks by Faye Martin, Rodale Press, Emmaus, PA, 1978. *A beautiful whole-foods classic.*

The New Laurel's Kitchen by Laurel Robertson, Carol Flinders, and Brian Ruppenthal, Ten Speed Press, Berkeley, CA, 1986. *A time-honored, whole-foods instructional cookbook.*

Sweet & Natural Desserts A compilation from the editors of East West Journal, 1986. *Wonderful whole-food recipes primarily using malt syrup or maple syrup.*

Sweet and Sugarfree by Karen E. Barkie, St. Martin's Press, New York, 1982. *This lovely book uses only fruit and fruit juices as sweeteners.*

The Ten Talents Cookbook by Frank and Rosalie Hurd, The College Press, Collegedale, TN, 1968. *A very complete natural foods and vegetarian cookbook.*

Tofu Cookery by Louise Hagler, Book Publishing Co., Summertown, TN, 1982. *Expert tofu cookery in a beautifully done book.*

SOURCES OF STEVIA PRODUCTS

Wisdom Herbs   (800) 899-9908
South American herbs, stevia products include: stevia tea bags, powdered leaf, white powdered extract, extract tablets, clear liquid extract, stevia liquid concentrate, stevia powdered extract with FOS filler. Free catalog   www.wisdomherbs.com *and* www.steviaplus.com

Nu Naturals, Inc.   (800) 753-4372
Stevia extracts in powder, liquid, tablets, packets. 2220 W. Second Avenue #1, Eugene, OR 97402 www.nunaturals.com

@Stevia LLC (888) 8-STEVIA
White powdered extract, powdered extract with filler in packets, and books. www.sweetvia.com

Jean's Greens   (888) 845-8327
White powdered extract, stevia leaves—powdered and cut and sifted, and books. Free catalog

Mulberry Creek Herb Farm   (419) 433-6126
Stevia leaf, starter plants in 3-inch pots. www.mulberrycreek.com

Seeds from Around the World   Jim Johnson   (800) 336-2064
Stevia seed kits   www.seedman.com

Park Seed Co.   (800) 213-0076
Stevia seeds.   www.parkseed.com

MAIL ORDER SOURCES FOR INGREDIENTS

Many of the starred (*) ingredients in the shopping list can be purchased by mail order, including stevia powder, carob powder, nut butters, soy and other specialty flours, soymilk powder, arrowroot, agar-agar, vegetarian gelatin, and nonaluminum baking powder.

Mail Order Catalog for Healthy Eating   (800) 695-2241
PO Box 180, Summertown, TN 38483
www.healthy-eating.com

BAKING EQUIPMENT SOURCES

Williams-Sonoma Company, San Francisco, CA
1-800-541-1262   Free catalog

Bridge Kitchenware, New York, NY
1-212-688-4220   Catalog $3

Sweet Celebrations, Minneapolis, MN
1-800-328-6722   Free catalog

Product Directory

Agar-agar: Imported by Eden Foods, Inc., Clinton, MI 49236   (517) 456-7424

Canoleo 100% Canola Margarine: Distributed by Spring Tree Corp., Brattleboro, VT 05302   (802) 254-8784

Earth Balance Natural Margarine: GFA Brands, Inc., PO Box 397, Cresskill, NJ 07626-0397   (201) 568-9300

Fruit Puree: There is a wonderful line of unsweetened fruit and berry purees called Fiordifrutta that is imported from Italy by Rigoni, Plantsville, CT 06479 Found in the jam section of the store, these purees can give your bakery variety and taste. You can use them to replace apple butter in cookies and bars. E-mail: rigoniusa@aol.com

Fruitsource: distributed by Advanced Ingredients, Inc., 1803 Mission St., Suite 404, Santa Cruz, CA 95060   (831) 464-9891. Now only sold in bulk.

Ginger Snaps, Vanilla Snaps, and Graham Crackers: MI-DEL brand, distributed by: American Natural Snacks, PO Box 1067, St. Augustine, FL 32085 MI-DEL makes whole grain graham crackers and nice ginger and vanilla snaps but they do contain sweetener. They are great for making a crumb crust.

Guar Gum: Bob's Red Mill Natural Foods, Inc., 5209 SE International Way, Milwaukie, OR 97222

Maple Flavoring: The Spicery Shoppe, Downers Grove, IL 60515   (630) 932-8100

Pomona's Universal Pectin: PO Box 1083, Greenfield, MA 01302 Pomona's Jam Hotline: (413) 772-6816

Stevia Concentrate and Stevia Tea Bags: These two stevia products may only be available from Wisdom Herbs. 1-800-899-9908.   www.wisdomherbs.com.

Vacuum-packed Tofu: Mori-Nu brand from Morinaga Nutritional Foods, PO Box 7969, Torrance, CA 90504   www.morinu.com

Vegetarian gelatin: Emes Kosher Products, Lombard, IL 60148

About the Author

Rita DePuydt is a free-lance botanist and writer, originally from Michigan, now living in California. She also has a background in Home-Economics and as a Medical Laboratory Technician.

Health and healing herbs have been an interest of hers for several decades. She was a leader in a nutrition education and activist group during her college years, was involved in her local food coop for several years, and has taught whole food vegetarian cooking classes.

Rita has been dealing with sugar sensitivity since a child. Following numerous ups and downs, she became interested in stevia as a way of reducing her consumption of sugars. She uses stevia and stevia extracts in all her baking, and stevia is an important part of her daily health program.

Rita is now learning that it's worthwhile to focus on what you want, not on what you don't want—to align your thoughts and feelings with what you really want. She believes that total health and happiness is within reach if you keep the vision and focus on the positive aspects.

Index

A

agar-agar 186, 188
Almond
    Delights 83
    Milk, Milkshake 34
almonds, about 180, 188
Apple
    Bran Muffins 44
    Butter 151, 181
    Cake 66-67
    Crisp 136-37
    Filling 158
    Mousse 145
    Pie 132-33
Applesauce 150-51
Applesauce Gingerbread 50
Apricot Sauce 155
arrowroot 185, 188

B

baked goods, storing 184
baking powder
    making 182
    testing 185
baking, high altitude 181
bananas
    Almond Milkshake 34
    Berry Ice Cream 173
    Bread 51
    Cake 78
    Coconut Cream Pie 120-22
    Coconut Custard 110
    Creamy Date Shake 33
    Date Pudding 112

bananas (cont.)
    freezing 181
    Orange Cooler 31
    Peanut Butter Banana Chocolate
        Chip Muffins 41
    Strawberry Pina Smoothie 29
    Summer Fruit Salad 143
Bars - See also Cookies
    Date 98
    Granola 100
    Peanut Butter 96
    Pumpkin 99
    Sesame Crisps 93
    Tropical Fruit 94-95
beverages
    hints for making 24
    Almond or Cashew Milk 34
    Cranberry Punch 28
    Ginger Ale 26
    Hot Carob Cocoa 35
    Hot Cocoa 36
    Lemonade 25
    Mint Stevia Iced Tea 25
    Orange Cooler 31
    Orange Pop 27
Biscuits, Yam Drop 54
Blackberry Cream Pie 126-28
Blueberry
    Muffins 42
    Pie 140
    Tofu Bundt Cake 72-73
bran 188
Bread, Quick
    Applesauce Gingerbread 50
    Banana 51
    Date Nut 49
    hints for making 38